IT
IS
WHAT
IT
IS

IT
IS
WHAT
IT
IS

MARIA FRANCISCUS

IT IS WHAT IT IS

iUniverse books may be ordered through booksellers or by contacting:

iUniverse
1663 Liberty Drive
Bloomington, IN 47403
www.iuniverse.com
844-349-9409

ISBN: 978-1-6632-2231-2 (sc)
ISBN: 978-1-6632-2232-9 (e)

Library of Congress Control Number: 2021908776

Print information available on the last page.

iUniverse rev. date: 04/29/2021

Based on a True
Experience of
Living in Poverty in Rural Ontario,
Single Parenthood of 4,
Mental Illness,
Sexual Assaults,
And
"Just–in-Case".

Names have been changed to allow for anonymity
Just-in case is an extra character that seems to
be (very often) in our companionship, more so
than in our compassion, in our realm of existence,
or perhaps is sent to simply to forewarn of the
nefarious Just-in–Time that makes his desires
known just when we are least accountable!!!!!

Via Con Dios
Maria

CHAPTER ONE

Sh-h-h, Listen I can hear the footsteps crossing the floor. His usual drag of one foot, then stops to catch up with the other foot. I freeze, unable to roll over to see if I tied the door handle to the bed frame. I tried my hardest to wake up when my Mom wakes up just to tie that door shut. But did I do it this morning? I am quivering in fear. I hate the outcome if I didn't get the door tied. I can't crawl under the bed because lots of boxes are stored there. I can't go out the window without breaking a leg. There is no-where to escape.

Not sure when I started sleeping with my mom. Dad slept downstairs on a daybed for as long as I can remember. With so many kids, there obviously was some together time.

Now that rope was my pride and joy. It was customary to use the baler twine after it came off the bales of hay to braid into an even stronger rope. The trick was to slice the twine where it was tied and you had a longer, smoother rope. Use it double and you had a *very* strong rope. I used the doubles. It was used for many additional purposes, such as a swing, calf tie ups, halters and practically anything you could imagine. There were lots of extra braided ropes for just-in-case!

Don't recall when I learned to braid but that too, was early in life. By tying the rope tight to my bedframe, no-one could open the door. The bed-frame was cast iron, and quite decorative and sturdy.

As an adult, I wonder why my mom never questioned why I had the rope there in the first place. I knew that if the door was tied, I was safe! Possibility was that she suspected and although denial made things go away in her mind, it did not in my reality! Her admonishment to stay away from him put the onus on me as a three year old child. That is an irrational demand but one taken seriously by a little child like me. So who would I tell? It felt like no-one on earth was invested in me. In fact where were, or who were my ports in the storms?

The shaping of being insignificant, worthless and unimportant began at an early age as it radiated daily to my soul and took up residence in the form of a small voice-"you are not worthwhile"..... It planted serious roots of doubt in the recesses of my mind. As an adult that is my first distress message: "You are not important. No-one cares about me."

Communication was non-existent unless it was gossip. We were on a party line of approximately sixteen homes. It was so hard to decipher whose ring it was with the combination of longs and shorts. Mind you, one could often tell be the way it rang, who was calling. Some had very little differentiation between longs and shorts. Five longs was the fire alarm.

My mom was an eavesdropper on all conversations as were half the neighbors. It wasn't called a party line for nothing! Woe upon us if we were noisy when my mother was "listening in." Once when my brother and I were bouncing around, she whacked me on top of the head with that heavy receiver. I swear the lights almost went out. Of course, I have no recollections of her favorite son ever getting reprimanded! Just-in-case you didn't notice that fact!

It is what it is.

We were not told as to why we had to get up out of bed at night when there were thunderstorms. As I grew older I realized it was just-in-case. The fear was the house would be hit by lightning and with no fast exit; we'd be roasted, baked or fried. I still dread thunderstorms because that fear was ingrained so young. Now it wasn't all pure anticipated fear. In reality, neighbors barns were hit by lightning, people were hit and it wasn't safe.

I've seen the lightning come through the phone line as a bright light or bounce off the wood stove. It was a real fear for all and especially for a child to see it happen. When there is an exceptionally loud crack of thunder, you knew something close had been hit. Naturally that fear continued into my present adulthood. Although I am getting better at not panicking when a storm is coming by. Counting the seconds between the end of the thunder to the first inkling of lightning gave an approximate distance of how far away the storm was. One second equaled one mile.

High winds scare me silly. In the hills or the countryside, a storm is much more pronounced in volume than in the suburbs. Yet I love the sound of thunder off in the distance, echoing through the hills. Slowly I am appreciating the lightning patterns.

When my kids were younger, ages 4, 6, 8 and 10 a storm was rolling through, so I huddled everyone to sit on the couch to wait it out. Now I am trying, oh so hard, not to show my apprehension. I look out the east window, and see the skies clearing. So I say, "Let's go upstairs to see how many windows were open enough to let the rain in." We just get to the top step when I hear the wind howling, and see an apple tree flying through the air. I instruct the kids to run quickly to the stairs at the other side of the house. They run. I hear the attached garage creaking, so instruct, "Quick run back to the other stairs." Once down stairs I see the barn roof flying towards the house, so I scream, "Quick get under the table." Then it is eerily quiet. My pulse is racing, my knees are shaking and I'm close to tears.

I am almost frozen in fear. I keep the kids inside. I don't know where to turn for help. The phone does not work, I look outside and the hydro wires are on the ground, and only five of the fourteen apple trees remain in the ground. The tree I seen flying in the air, left a crater in my garden and landed on the highway. Our poor bunny had flown over the house in his wire cage, and yet survived. Two huge pines were partially toppled, but when trying to upright them with the tractor, it was futile. The power of wind! What carnage to behold. My first tornado! I'm furious my husband Petrus, had not come home for support. Apparently at his family farm, there was only a small storm.

Yet through all this, I love trees. I need trees. Trees are my safety. When I was being sexually assaulted, I would escape to the bush to nurse my hurts, anger and fears. Technically some folks call it a forest, but it was the bush to me. To have the bush to hide in was an incredible sense of safety, seclusion and oblivion for me.

Consequently, I still plant many trees on my property much to the chagrin of my neighbor. He claims they interfere with his satellite dish reception. They do, but he could easily raise his dish up to aim it skywards. I'd plant the trees and inadvertently the kids would mow them off. My aim is to get a variety of trees. I love the catalpa tree best of all. Once I started charging the kids a dollar a tree they slowed down in mowing them off! My magnolia tree didn't survive the drought this summer, so when my grandson mowed it off, he just argued it was a stick. Well it was my stick!! Hopefully it will resurface again next spring. I NEED my trees!

My perpetrator always threatened to kill me if I said anything so escaping to the bush was my safety plan. That statement alone would suggest that he knew what he was doing was wrong. As I aged, the feelings were conflictual. I knew what was happening was wrong but stimulation of the clitoris was a good feeling. How could that be?

I had re-occurring nightmares, always dreaming of escape plans and a social sense of anxiety. I wanted to run away. There wasn't much opportunity to really get away or for any length of time - like forever. Once I took the centre out of the woodpile that was allotted for the sugar camp. Using boards for supports I made myself a little camouflaged cubbyhole and stocked it with apples, carrots and other garden supplies and books, just-in-case. I'd spend the day hiding out till after dark. No-one enquired where I had been. After all, I was the troubled emotional teen.

I've been coached that for Post-Traumatic Stress Disorder, (PTSD) the recommendation is to ground yourself and visualize something gentle, calm and soothing. No problem- I can easily see myself at water's edge, holding down the head of my perpetrator under water. Deep breathe - All is okay. Relaxing and I'm in control!!!

That exercise can be expanded in suspense by describing the soft, yet granular sand filtering between your toes, the gentle wind blowing through your hair, the aroma of a multitude of flowers sifting through the nostrils and yes, visualize anybody who has ticked you off!

It is what it is.

When I think of my safety ports, my oldest sister comes to mind. Her oldest was 21 days younger than me so we bonded well. That had its advantageous benefits at times of conflict. She and her family arriving on weekends gave a strong sense of belonging and safety mixed with opportunities. We played together and went on picnics to the lake. A sense of normalcy prevailed during the visits. She always provided Easter/Christmas treats like I had never seen before. As kids we made Easter baskets from empty dish detergent bottles. We were forever saving things long before recycling became a fad.

I will never forget her hubby trying and succeeding in catching a baby skunk. It became their household pet. Man did he stink after being sprayed my mama skunk!

CHAPTER TWO

I did not hail from a wealthy or even from a modest family. We had no hydro- no indoor plumbing and none of the sequential amenities like TV, bathtub/shower or mixer to bake with. I was really in the dark about life outside the home. Other neighbors had electricity, but my dad was against it. I never understood until much later in life how my neighbor watched her soap. What is exciting about watching a box of Tide, Sunlight or whatever the brand was? No excitement there for me.

Everything was done by hand. Turning the grindstone to sharpen the axe or the scythe was a weekly task of mine. Carrying water from the well, then the pump was done several times a day. Of course, I think, we all got our fingers or hands caught in the wringer of the gas powered washing machine. Why we hung clothes out on the line in winter to only bring in these frozen items to dry by the wood stove pipes never made sense to me.

I clearly recall the time when a grade eight student came tearing into the school house at the closing time. John F Kennedy was shot and killed. I had no idea who he was. The resulting frenzy from the teacher and older students was frightening. It was big news. News I wasn't kept abreast off. Mind you this also meant I was exempt from the TV monopoly on coverage of the event. Same thing, when Dean Martin died. I figured I was related to Martin's so this must be a relative. I was naive in current events.

Along with all the poverty, it was natural all my clothes were second hand. Oh, the joy when my older cousin was coming with her daughter's cast offs! Clothes were always recycled. New did not exist. With a family of eight kids, and the youngest two having a ten yr. gap to the next oldest: the dynamics were like a second family.

It was immensely unsettling when Allan and I learned our Aunt had three illegitimate children. One daughter, that had just been located was on the way to meet us. We were roughly ten and eleven. It made us wonder and worry if we were adopted? Remember that little communication existed and our fears were never addressed. Such secrets were typical in those days and especially so entrenched in our family. Women were not referenced as "pregnant" they were referred to as "in the family way"... Terminology was obscure. The more obscure usually meant the more negative inference. That fear of secrecy and obscurity still resonates in my soul 60+ years later. I loathe it.

Years later or more accurately she just got the results from a Ancestry DNA test and was over the moon in excitement. Those step siblings were bouncing with excitement to meet her. A 75 year old aunt knew the entire story. I want to be a fly on the wall to hear the exchange between them! As much as she inquired about family dynamics, I had no inkling. It was long before my time.

It is what it is.

I have vivid memories of seeing the drunk neighbor entering into the summer kitchen and accosting my mom with a butcher knife. She'd tell us kids to go upstairs until she came and got us. Quite a time would go by. I often wondered whose child am I. A recent Ancestry DNA test indicates my older sister is my sister, so all must be kosher. The doc told my mom she was going through menopause and 9 months later, there I was! She popped another child a year later. I never knew of my older siblings to live at home. Perhaps four of us kids lived at one time in the house. The others had married and moved out in my recollections. I was "shelved" at birth. No crib or cradle for me. I was kept in a dresser drawer! When I went onto cow's milk, I bawled and bawled. The older sister who looked after me more than my mom, never fails to remind me how she paced the floor night after night with me, trying to settle me. Today we know I have a milk allergy but back then you winged it.

It took until adulthood to learn of my allergies. I love tomatoes. I'd have them for breakfast, lunch and supper plus snack. Every September I'd end up in hospital with severe asthma. To find out I was allergic to tomatoes was not comprehendible. But indeed I am, so I simply limit the consumption to once a day. If I get asthmatic, I back off.

Sons were the desired outcome and more than once my dad let me know that. He would tell me to put my thumb on a nail he was hammering, and then hammer it. He'd just say "If you were a boy you wouldn't be so stupid," I'd just cry and my older sister would just say, "It didn't hurt that bad- did it?" Yes it did hurt, plus I was scared. What was I to do? If I didn't follow his directive, there was the leather strap to deal with. Actually it was a piece of the harness from the horses. He kept it behind the old cupboard in the summer kitchen. One day in my early teens, that strap went "missing". Everyone questioned why the fire smelt so bad this one particular day. It must have been wet wood- lol. The strap was history!!!!!

It is what it is.

I strive to teach my grandkids the difference between discipline and abuse. Society's pendulum has swung so far that now the parents are afraid to discipline. The slightest touch and the kids are quick to scream abuse. I also want them to learn that with every right there is an equal responsibility. You have the right to free speech but you have the responsibility to ensure your words do not hurt anyone and are deemed responsible in the household. That acceptance may differ from household to household but at Grandma's certain expressions and words, including lyrics are taboo.

Back to my childhood house, it was a log cabin with an upstairs and down, and a summer kitchen. The upstairs was divided into two rooms. In the cold of winter, you wrapped your clothes around the stovepipe to warm them before putting them on! The water would freeze in the house. You had to break the ice in the morning to get a drink from the pail or to get washed. Cold was an understatement!! Being cold terrifies me. My worst nightmare would is to be homeless in the cold.

It wasn't that uncommon for the pipes to go on fire. The creosol built up and ignited. The pipes would be red hot. Mom started cleaning the pipes once a month, to reduce the chance of fire. Once in the summer, apparently a spark drifted into the attic of the summer kitchen catching the roof on fire. It was so scary. All I wanted was my doll but I wasn't allowed in. Eventually the neighbors got the fire out and the house was intact. I retrieved my doll.

You learned to cook everything on the wood stove. It was a challenge to keep the temperature even for baking or cooking the meals. Yet my mom was capable of producing really good food. Cooking in the summer was insufferable. Most of my early cooking mistakes were made in the kitchen and someone had to eat them! Burnt cookies were common.

Ironing clothes on a hot summer day by heating up the iron on the wood stove was murder but it was one of my favorite chores. I often would set the ironing board up outside!

Every day after changing from my school clothes it was; get a snack, and then go out to bring in wood for the night, and help put the cows in the barn with feed and sileage. During maple syrup season I had the cattle to look after. That I enjoyed. After supper it was taking the gas lantern down to the barn so my mom could see to milk the cows. My dad never milked the cows. The cows kicked him so much so that he couldn't. The job fell to me if my mom couldn't be there.

Once holding the lantern in the barn, I felt my leg and foot get warm and warmer. Darn little calf was peeing down my boot! It was so common to squirt the cats or my brother by tilting the cow's teat and letting the milk go!

We kept the extra milk or cream down in the well where it was cool. Climbing down in was always fun. How we never actually fell in was a blessing. The jagged rocks provided a substantial foot and hand hold. The milk can was tied to a rope (made from baler twine) and lowered into the cool water until the milk truck came.

Another job I enjoyed was to be the nanny for a sow and her piglets. It was my duty to stay in her pen, making sure she did not lay on any of the little ones. How exciting!

One of the worst jobs was doing my dad's feet. He would soak them in a pan of water, and then demand me into esthetic service. Using a jack knife, I was to pare down the dead skin after drying the feet, and then I had to add this Watkins or Raleigh's cream. He often would have deep cracks that required a tender touch. Many times the air was blue because I was not careful enough. Oh how I cringed knowing I was going to be cursed something terrible for not doing the job just so. Where was my kid brother for his turn in doing this???? Or my mom?

Another grossness I endured was the keeping of dead beavers, muskrats or otters under the wood stove in the kitchen or main room. They needed to thaw out so my dad could skin them. Gosh I detested that!! Presumably the money from furs validated the work involved.

Nor was I into hunting season. The carcass of deer or moose sickened me. I hate the thoughts of the poor animal being shot. Most of the family liked the meat but I could not stomach it. I have an active brain and a weak, reactive stomach. My dad savored the organ meats. I never could hack the look of liver, the smell of liver, or the taste of liver. Today it still repulses me.

In my younger years we also had the travelling bread man. Can you visualize five loaves for a dollar!!!!. Sometimes my brother and I were allowed to get a Twinkie, Joe Louis. We then create a treasure hunt for each other.

A fond memory was going to the neighbor's house once after school. I can still see us sitting on her sofa, with a TV tray, fresh white bread bologna sandwich and a glass of cold milk while watching TV. Awesome!!!

Maybe I am a PITA- (**P**ain **I**n **T**he **A**ss)

It is what it is.

CHAPTER THREE

Growing up and living in an isolated rural location, meant friends were few and chores were plentiful. We got bikes when my oldest sister's boys outgrew theirs. Sometimes we got the use of the tractor to go visit my sister, but most times it was shank's mare that got us to point A and back.

One year we had to walk down through the fields and bush to school, regardless of rain, sleet, or snow. It was so much fun dropping in to Auntie's where we got treats of sugar cookies before school. Her kids had already left to be on time for school. My bro and I, grade 4 & 5, trudged daily, singing loudly to scare away bears.

Whoops, one Tuesday following Thanksgiving my bro was silently making the trek alone when he rounded a clump of cedars to encounter a bear rearing up, and growling. It then ran off in one direction and Allan to the opposite. It is difficult to say who was most scared- the bear or him? I chose a good day to be sick. Perhaps we would have been noisier if the two of us were attending and the event wouldn't have happened. A Thanksgiving does not go by without me remembering that event.

My poor aunt had a bear in her cellar basement once, examining her preserves. There was an outside entrance that some-one had left open. Bears were forever making their presence known. I was in the outhouse, when one unbeknownst to me, passed just metres away on its way to the turkey pen.

Walking that path to school and back, was also retaliation time with my younger brother. I would run ahead and throw rocks at the bee's nest hanging from the tree just so he'd get stung. I turned out to be the one allergic to bees. At the end of grade 13, I was getting a dress hemmed by my sister at her house when I went unconscious. Rushed to the hospital, it revealed little more than what we already knew. I had been stung on the end of my long finger on my left hand the previous day at 2 p.m. My arm swelled up to the elbow. It was exactly 24 hours later that I konked out.

Honey bee and bumble bees have the same type of venom. My dad kept honey bees, extracting the honey for us and for sale. Now today I own an acre of land. There are acres and acres of farmland around me. You tell me why a bee must come into my house? It comes into my kitchen. It sets itself down at my place at the table. Its stinger is ready. Too bad a bottle of Tylenol three's sees to its demise by fervently squishing it!

Do unto others as they do unto you! They kill me: I kill them first.

Swarms of bees are something to see. How they make this cone-shaped swirling mass that can travel quite a distance. It is a marvel. It is a beekeeper's dream to capture one and expand the existing colonies. There is an unspoken code of ethics that you call the nearest apiary to see if they "lost" a colony. When a hive gets too big, a queen bee will rally the troops to fly off to make a new home, especially if another queen bee has hatched.

You never react to your first bee sting. I certainly had my share growing up. Each reaction got worse than the previous one. The venom builds up and one day your body reacts negatively. It can be fatal.

Only I would get stung by a bee in January, the midst of winter in Ontario. I was in the grocery store where I grabbed a cart. I promptly got stung on the hand by a bee! And it is only me who puts on a pair of rubber duckies that result in me getting stung on the toe. It is only me who, watches a bee's nest on the roof of the shed and seeing no action knocks it down with a hockey stick. One bee! Just one bee catapults out of the nest! One bee that lands on my arm and proceeds to sting me! Do I have a death wish? I don't think so but Freud would probably argue.

Our mother always told us to stand still if a bee is around us. One time, my poor brother was standing on a rock that had a wasp nest under it. He is screaming with the stings while my mother is screaming at him to run. What a commotion. He finally ran and other than some swelling, redness and soreness, he fared well.

It was priceless to listen to my young granddaughter argue with the minister's ideology to be nice to all God's little creatures including insects. She staunchly corrected him that bees kill Grandma, so we must kill them first!

CHAPTER FOUR

During my childhood, I never moved once, yet switched schools three times depending on the school board's decisions about busing. For busing to school, you had to be three miles from the school. We were 1/10th a mile short.

So we either walked to school or since the school bus driver for the next county lived one mile from our mailbox, the instructions were to be bussed to the other county's public or high school. Some years we walked to his place, other years got picked up or a combination thereof. Sometimes the generosity of the bus driver meant we got picked up in the morning and walked home.

In forty some years of sending kids to school, only once did my mom sleep in. That morning the driver drove right into our yard. We were still sleeping!

The bus driver and his wife kept us supplied in eggs; so many times we carried them home along with our school books. With no back packs we literally carried the binders, pencil cases, math sets and books in our arms. We didn't have a pencil sharpener so used a paring knife to sharpen pencils.

One summer my cousin, my brother and I walked over to those neighbours to get the weekly order of two dozen eggs. They had a temperamental dog. At the first sign of growling, the other pair took off running through the yard before I got started. That dog grabbed me by the right leg. I still sport the scars. The dog met his waterloo that night. Dogs, big or small, still frighten me.

That same man was drunk at a fair dance when he commented on my athletic build. That is discreet for saying flat chested. He was more graphic about how he had bigger boobs than me. I developed an uneasy feeling about him. I didn't trust him. Since my brother and I were first to be picked up and last to be dropped off, I felt safe with my brother on the bus. When alone, I was fearful. He never tried anything on the bus. Thank God.

He did have a habit of stopping to chat with a neighbor leaving us to be at least a good half hour late in getting home. Thank goodness we could read or do homework during his lull in duties!

Riding the bus was an experience for sure. If the bus got "stuck" in the morning, the older boys would get off and fake pushing until the driver announced it was after 9 then they buckled down. There was a thrill to being late for school. On the way home it was the opposite- immediate pushing. Imagine a busload of all ages, no cell phone and icy roads. No such things as snow days. The chains went on, and the bus rolled on. Only once in my memory did the evening buses fail to make it. It was ice rain and roads were skating rinks! Boys slept in the gym and girls in the cafeteria. Hot dogs for supper, breakfast and lunch!!!

It wasn't cool to wear snow pants in high school, so we would shove them under the school bus seats until dismissal time. We donned them for the cold trek in the laneway. Now mind you, girls had to wear dresses for many years to school. I recall in grade nine when a few rebels wore slacks under the dresses. Thankfully the day arrived when girls could wear pants!! Gone were the nylons, garter belts and eventually those belts for sanitary pads.

School life was strange. In one of the upper grades I was so bored in the Marketing class; the teacher gave me the job of teaching it. I did and did it well but did not get his salary.

Incidentally, four years later studying journalism at university I loved learning about subliminal advertising. On a New Year's Eve toboggan party my nephew crashed into a frozen cow dung patty, breaking his finger. We sat in the hospital waiting room discussing the ads in the magazine pointing out the subliminal messages. We swore up and down no one was drinking. When we left we glanced backwards in time to see the doctor checking out the ads!!!

The following year the principal expelled me because of some letter I wrote during the summer cursing and criticizing the school. Now he could not produce the letter when my dad insisted. The school board made him apologize and re-instate me. My dad being so angry retaliated by keeping me out longer. Guess who was caught in the center??? That whole scenario was weird and I knew I had not written such a letter. Cursing was not my style.

CHAPTER FIVE

S tarting school was daunting to a child that was so shy; I didn't even talk in front of house guests. Strange how we girls had to always wear a kerchief. The prettiest kerchiefs were the ones from my Scotland relatives. This head covering protected our ears, I guess. My neighbor drove me to school in her car since there was no bus service at that time. Once we were hit by another vehicle on a sharp corner. Having no seatbelt mandates, I bounced off the dash. Definitely I was more frightened than hurt for sure.

Life in a rural one room school house had a story of its own. It was heated with a wood stove. Outhouse style washrooms were two seaters just off the entrance to the classroom. This particular school did not have a basement, so the wood stove was at the back of the classroom. All grades were in the same room. The teacher was housed with a neighbor.

In one school, a grade eight student went down to the basement to fill the stove with wood. Try to convince me he didn't have his text book down there to check information for the test he was writing! We were more than toasty when he kept stoking the fire!!!

I failed my first year (grade 1 then) in school, because I wouldn't talk to the teacher or in the classroom. Outside I laughed and played with my peers who were mainly cousins. Report card was A's and F's. Anything verbal, I would not open my mouth, so naturally I failed.

The second year I was put in the corner for talking! Still today I am irked about that- I was simply listening to the boy ahead and the one behind me jabber-jab. Thanks Donnie and Delbert. To talk or be quiet is always my dilemma! To combat this shyness, I was bribed with Canadian Tire money if I would interact with the teacher. It didn't work. Throughout grade and high school, the teachers kept saying I should talk more in group settings. Today I am uncomfortable with silence and feel I need to say something. Consequently I am often elected to be the one to speak up and in fact, addressed for comments. It is un-nerving to say the least. I do remain competent in response.

Ironically, in grade eight I won the public speaking contest much to the surprise of the elementary teacher who failed me in first grade. It was so hilarious to watch the principal double over- yes totally double over, when I spoke of my involvement in 4-H and how we learned such things as "Don't milk a cow during a thunderstorm: she may be struck by lightning and you would be left holding the bag!.

In high school, I was asked to coach the younger students during public speaking competitions. How do you coach public speaking? So much for hand index cards or cues. I sweat so badly the ink ran. Just memorize and go for it. Keep your eyes circulating the crowd and keep an eye on the clock. So many parents just wrote the speeches without the student having zero recollection of what they were saying. Never have your parent contribute beyond grammatical concepts. Even today I remain very conscientious of the um's when people speak. The speech has to be your words so it flows naturally from you. Choose a topic you are interested in.

Once in the early grades, I had my mom help me with math- addition and subtraction. 40- wrong because she added instead of subtracting. She was fired from that job never to have a second go. Humiliation- 40 wrong!!!!! Not that math was my strong suite; it was incorrigible to have 40 wrong (out of 40 questions).

The older girls would comb my hair as we listened to the teacher read an afternoon story following lunch hour. I only had short hair but they loved to put bows and ribbons in it. It was great to be pampered. Friday was either art day or a movie on the old reel. The teacher had all eight grades to teach, monitor and instruct through the various subjects. Again even though I didn't talk, I listened, and retained knowledge.

One day my bladder just couldn't wait till bathroom time, but no way was I asking to go to the washroom. Standing in front of the class for some subject lesson, the flood came-the older girls did the clean-up...

It is what it is.

If we gathered butternuts in the fall, we had to have a note from the parents to explain our yellow fingers; otherwise we were believed to have been smoking. Leeks in the springtime would drive everyone whacko with the pungent smell on lunches. Some were sent outside to eat and mouthwash was available for afterwards. There is nothing worse than the smell of leeks. Well, maybe sardines!!!

For those of us who sought out the morels, the spring mushroom, we fared better. The spring warmth followed by rain meant a good crop. Some people like my brother and older sister, had a natural ability to find them. You soaked them in salt water overnight, then sautéed in butter to serve over toast for breakfast!

Down through the years, the challenge was who had the first ripe tomato. My understanding is that the day my one sister was born at home, my mom went to the garden to pick things for a salad that same afternoon. Yes, there was the first ripe tomato. The competition still exists.

It is what it is...

CHAPTER SIX

Bullying existed for sure in my childhood, and I'm embarrassed to say I was part of the problem. In my defense, I was not the instigator. We were seated three per seat. It was a mixture of public and high school students. There was a youngster assigned to sit with myself and another gal who was two years my junior. That fellow high school girl would not move over in the seat to give the little tyke any room. Poor thing was from a struggling family, and never raised a fuss. When it was just her and I, we engaged in some talk about school, friends etc. I wonder where she is today. Why did I not insist?

But then I was a victim of bullying as well especially throughout the high school years. An older girl, say older by a year, had it in for me. She constantly sat behind me on the bus, mimicking everything I said or did, and included an exaggerated "tsk" and sighing sound. How intimidating!! It fed into my reservations about talking. Silent I remained.

When it was hillbilly dress up day: she didn't dress up and yet mocked my clothes as being my everyday choice. She was a bully. Her cousin aided and abetted her.

The inner tears drowned my soul.

My mom thought her mom was just super lady so I couldn't disclose. Her mom was super nice as was her brother and dad. Who could I share with?

Even today I just cringe at the resurgence of feelings thinking of those days. Why can't I forget?

When I was grade 1 or 2, I had the three girls over for my birthday party. Just really nothing planned in terms of activities, but had them over anyways. I was in the woodshed crying when my mom said if I didn't stop crying I would never have another party. She did not ask the reason for my tears. I had heard the three of them discussing how poor I was!!! That was the end of my get-togethers for my birthday. I was so hurt!!

In those days, the birthday cake had coins wrapped up in the centre icing. That was a treat. So not only was I afraid to have sleepovers in case of ridicule of poverty, but deadly afraid they too would be sexually assaulted!

Later in life, I hosted a shin-dig to celebrate my retirement, burning of the mortgage, successful knee replacement and having successfully as a single parent raised four young adults. Two of my own kids did not attend and one other was positive no-one would show. There were over 200 attendees. My one and only party was a fun time. Why do my own kids discredit me when I made so many sacrifices for them? It tears the heart out of me. Why? Why? why?

My brother got to go trick or treating with his school chum Cal, while I stayed home. Sometimes he shared his pillowcase full of candies. Halloween usually consisted of the older kids damaging mailboxes with a bat, overturning outhouses or re-locating farm machinery. We were far enough off the track, we usually escaped those antics. I never developed a keen interest in Halloween. I felt left out and alone.

I taught the Sunday school kids that although they are behind a mask- God sees you!

It is what it is.

CHAPTER SEVEN

Our lane way alone was 9/10ths of a mile long so we relied on the neighbor woman to phone to say when the mail had gone by. I routinely walked my 4-H calf out to get the mail. Those days, often groceries were sent from the village general store to the individuals' mailbox and you squared up the next time you went to "town". Going to town, as a child meant you got dressed up in dresses for us females with white socks and shiny shoes. For me who preferred barefoot, that was a challenge. So many times I cut my foot or toes badly, and my dad would curse me for not wearing shoes. My oldest sister was the same. Time and time again she showed up with her family and no shoes!!! I could walk across freshly mowed hayfields with no issues. Oh yes, when we got thistles in our feet, across my mom's knees we would go while she dug them out. Ouch!!!

With so many young nieces and nephews, I was surrounded by children. Now as an early teen I had to go to babysit my sister's kids while she shopped. I would get in exchange a 5 cent vanilla Dairy Queen ice-cream cone or maybe- just maybe, go the restaurant. There I could choose fries **or** a burger. We certainly had no McDonalds' or other fast food joints. Her hubby sometimes sneaked a dollar or two if I babysat at night. Those days the vehicle had a sheet of plywood across the back seat up to the front seats and kids played. No car seats or restraints required. Children had space to move about or even lay down for a snooze.

Once when they went out I was playing hide and go seek with the three kids, I thought it was wise to hide in the bathtub. Oh dear. I never thought the tub would be wet!!! Again, I had no tub at home so no reference point! We had sponge baths. I never used the showers after gym class simply because I didn't know how to operate them.

When my siblings were getting groceries for my mom, she averaged a dollar for every item. She also collected the Gold Bond stamps. The items she redeemed the stamps for were usually for bridal, baby or wedding gifts. What a thrill to paste the tiny stamps on the booklet pages. And to collect those porcelain animal figurines in the Red Rose tea bag boxes! Those figurines are worth a few dollars today!

I had a dear aunt, my mother's sister whom I loved to bits. She was super sweet and quiet like me. (LOL) She also had lots of kids with one just 21 days older than me. That poor dear was predeceased by five of her ten children. What a load for her to carry.

Before that aunt moved to that last location where she lived, she lived closer to my first rural school where so many of my cousins attended. Her hubby, a war veteran died young. This was at a time when wakes were held in the house. Oh, my gosh, we were in attendance and being bored, us four younger ones, we chose to play hide and go seek in the house at night. Today I cringe when I recall her youngest daughter and me hiding under the casket drape!!! Since "it" person couldn't find us we started untying shoe laces as folks paid respect. Did we get a lickin' for that!!! How did we not topple the casket? As an adult I am aghast I did such a thing!

Her one daughter was notorious for ending up at our place. I recall her always in a yellow dress. She would hide down in the seats of the bus, and the driver figured he let all the kids off and on we went. She was fun and no-one seemed to mind she came over.

It is what it is!

CHAPTER EIGHT

I truly wasn't a violent person but I seemed to have a couple of lads strongly believing I was going to kill them. One was my cousin from up north. They had come down for a visit and I took a VERY strong dislike to him. At the Sunday gathering at my brother's place I chased him around and around the honeysuckle tree/bush. I got him on the ground, straddling him, and pinning his arms with my knees before pummeling him with my fists. That did not go over well with the adults. To this day he says he thought he was going to die and I tell him that was my intentions!!! Now when he gets rowdy I just ask if I need to take a round out of him again. Probably since 1978 we became friends and close like cousins should be!

The other chap can fondly tell you how he also thought he was going to die at my hands. In high school, my home economics knitting project was knitting a vest, beret and scarf. Time was running out so I was knitting the scarf almost to conclusion on the bus when this dear lad pulled my knitting needle, knocking all my stitches off!!! Luckily my mom rescued the stitches and I was able to finish the project on time. He spent all summer trying to make up by buying me hot dogs and chocolate bars at ball games. Was he really just attempting to flirt? He flirted with murder as the outcome if I had my way!!!! When I met his wife, the first thing she said was "oh you are the one who taught him not to touch knitting needles!" Yes, I could have killed him.

Perhaps he is just doomed when it comes to knitting needles. Recently he sucked up his wife's knitting in the vacuum. He tries but just can't learn to avoid knitting at all costs. Good job he is away trucking most times. Today he is a good friend. He was instrumental in getting my son, George into trucking.

It is what it is.

Although I studied hard, achieved well, school had its disappointments. I'd make the track team or sports teams but had to bail because I had no transportation. I so enjoyed the house league games. I never went to prom or school dances.

In 1967, the grades 7 & 8 were going to Expo in Montreal and for some reason there was one extra ticket. There was a draw of us grade 6 students. My name was pulled. I was so thankful my parents let me go. Sometimes I wonder if that was staged. Did my name really get selected or was it set up?? Regardless it was a fantastic experience. So I guess sometimes I got to participate in some things.

There was a 30 mile walkathon that I really wanted to do. My dad sponsored me with so much for the first ten miles, then so much more for the next ten miles, then more for the final 10 miles. I was the first girl in. That night I went to a wedding reception and danced all night. The next day I was so-o-o sore and tired.

I guess that is why I make sure I am involved in my kid's school lives. I always went to concerts, interviews etc. I never wanted them to feel as badly as I did. Now I question, why there are no pictures of me at their events but pictures only with their dad and Oma. They tell me it is because I am always there. That's good?

It is what it is!

CHAPTER NINE

At school I was mostly a loner- high marks, withdrawn and reserved- all the classic indicators of an abused child, yet no-one intervened. I use to cry and pray God would send me to the Children's Aid Society (CAS). One high school math teacher asked me if everything was okay at home but quickly retracted by saying to forget it, he didn't want to get involved. Now by law they must intervene. Some changes are good.

As a teen, I was plagued with vaginal infections, although neither the doc nor my mom supposedly clued in that something was amiss. Perhaps they simply chose to overlook.

I developed an ulcer and was sent to Kingston to a psychologist for counselling after a week of hospitalization. When he asked my parents to attend they refused. By the way, I went to my appointments when a neighbor was taking their own child to medical appointments. That was scary and emotional because I didn't really know them.

Interestingly enough, I suffered a concussion vaulting over the wooden horse at gym class, I was sent by ambulance to the hospital over an hour way. No parental visit. I was discharged to my cousin's until my older brother came to retrieve me.

Had my appendix removed and thanks to neighbor Lorne who happened to be in the doctor's office, ended up at the hospital. No parental visit.

Following year had my tonsils out. No parental visit.

Had a knee cartilage surgery and my aunt, a registered nurse from out of the country, happened to be there to see me through. No parental visit.

Again the message of me not being important was loud and clear. As a parent now, I cannot fathom how they could have been so detached. True my mom did not drive but....

The knee surgery was so hilarious because the gym teacher also had surgery for same reason. We did the two-crutch shuffle for winter carnival. Now that surgery was the second try. The first trip to the operating room, the surgeon was going to operate on the wrong knee. How he was stopped I don't know. Luckily someone did stop him. The following day, I taped a huge sign on my leg so there would be no mistake.

Man, the cast was up to my crotch so I thought they had cut my leg off! Then I had a jerk for a nurse. They were to slowly lift my leg up and down. She lifted my leg and dropped it. Yup, that pain was excruciating!

Now to call someone a bitch seems important, but as I counselled folks- look at it this way. Bitch means:

B-beautiful
I-Intelligent
T-talented
C- caring
H- helpful

Doesn't hurt so much anymore-eh? Reactions are based on interpretations, so take the high road!!!

It is what it is.

CHAPTER TEN

From the rural school days, I made some real nice friends with whom I still connect today. It was just ghastly when Catherine admitted she did not wear underwear beneath her dress that day when she was in grade 4!!! Now the friends are scattered across the country. My high school seat buddy is in British Columbia and we recently connected.

Many times I wonder about my former classmates and their whereabouts. I regret not being more forward because there was the corporal's son I had a major crush on. Beyond a "hi" when we passed from classes, I could not bring myself to pursue him.

My crush in grade school was allowed to come to our house for a sleepover on the premise he was a guest of my bro Allan. He and I had a falling out that seemed appropriate to settle by climbing the two trees behind the school wood shed. We scampered up, only to get up quite a distance up, like near the top, and then we looked down to see the teacher shaking her finger at us with promises of the strap. He and I looked at each other; decided if we stayed up there she couldn't get us. You know I have no recollection of coming down that tree- am I still up there? Am I in another stratosphere? Guess what? Ironically you are here with me!!!!

It is what it is.

There were two older boys in the school of whom the oldest was not very nice. Some of their suggestive behaviors were far from anything I had knowledge of. That was weird!

One day the older of the lads, grabbed me in front of the school, out of sight of the teacher, and put his hands in my pants. Having him finger me was scary and when an older cousin came running back to get me, only then did he push me away. A game of hide & go seek, hopscotch, red rover, farmer in the dell, ring-around the rosy, what time is it Mr. Wolf, duck, duck goose, tag, frozen tag, baseball, soccer, fox and the goose in winter, would get us all interacting. There were lots of laughs to make one forget the bad things in life. Of course, I told no-one about what happened but wondered why me again? Life in a one room school house meant no-one said anything about anything. Again secrets prevailed. I loathe obscurity and secrets. No good comes from being that way.

The music teacher travelled from school to school so the boys, of course, tied a snake to the gate so he wouldn't come into the school. Whether he untied the snake or the snake slithered undone, we still had music class. Those old favorites- Green Beret, My Grandfather's clock, Via Con Dios, seasonal classics, and my favorite song- "Mary had a little lamb".

I loved feeding the orphan lambs. It was easy to feed three at a time. A bottle in each hand and one between my knees and I was in business.

We had one sheep that lambed triplets early in the season. Believing one was dead; my dad tossed it aside until he got the other two nursing. Me being me, but me being contrary in my dad's expectations, I was quite sure it still had life. I bundled it up to bring back to the house.

There, I put it in a straw-lined box in the oven part of the wood stove. I kept the stove stoked at a medium heat all night. I kept giving it tastes of rum off my finger, massaging it gently until it bleated at 3 a.m. I whooped in celebration, waking up the entire household, much to the chagrin of my dad. My dad was so sure that the lamb was a lost cause. I think everything I did was a lost cause to him simply because I was a girl. The lamb survived and became one of my bottle fed pets.

I sure learned the hard way to never get between a mother ewe and her lamb nor in fact don't get between a cow and her calf. It was by natural survival training, I got to be a runner and good in high jump, hurdles and the dash. Many pounds ago I was a cross country runner.

On occasion the bull would get loose in his stall. I would open the door and he'd come charging out. Again a speedy exit was required. Most times the bull was docile but we were taught not to play Russian roulette with him.

Another bottle fed lamb was growing quite robustly when he broke his leg at the knee. There is no fixing a broken sheep leg, even with splints. That guy could motor. He usually followed my 4-H calf or spent time butting heads with the bull. Well he became quite interested in wee 3 year old Stan, chasing him around and around the house as fast as both could go on their legs. All we hear is Stan's cries for help as he bolts through the open screen door. The lamb goes right under the kitchen table to get a shot at butting the poor child. It was to no avail, as wee Stan was ousted onto his dad's knee and the lamb was escorted back to the barnyard. The table was being moved by this lamb so it had to be righted, and my dad's teacup replenished. To this day I will not eat lamb in any way, shape or form.

They are my darlings.

My love.

My passion.

Not my supper!

CHAPTER ELEVEN

Fortunately, I was able to participate in both agricultural and homemaking 4-H clubs. Having a brother who was a leader made transportation possible then. When I learned to drive, I went to the homemaking clubs. My sister attended many homemaking clubs, but how did she get rides? Hm.m.m...

It is what it is.

Getting back to agricultural 4-H component, our 4-H meetings involved recreation organized by myself. Usually, we often played baseball. This older, majorly cute guy was teasing me by not allowing me to get the bat. He swung it back and forth in front of his body, just out of my reach. Well now I reached and grabbed- yikes not the bat but his pants and the contents within!!! I was just as embarrassed as he was!

I still think he is so handsome. I went out west for my pen pal's wedding and he greeted me at the airport. I was not expecting this. This "cowboy" kept getting in my way and I kept saying, "Excuse me." Finally I recognized him under his big Stetson! He had arranged accommodation at his married friend's home.

This pen pal remains my friend today. We started corresponding after I read her ad in the Winnipeg Free Press. Then it was paper and pen, now emails. To go to her wedding was so great and she came to my graduation! Several other penpals dropped off after a time, but this one was so special.

Thanks to him, there were many personalized tours around the area including the Hot Springs in Banff. Interestingly, he was instrumental in leading me to accept Christ as my Savior.

On the return trip to Ontario, it was quite the sight to see a saddle on the turnstile with luggage. When this man grabbed it, I asked if the horse was coming next. Yep I'm shy!!!

In the Homemaking section of 4-H, we made many different dishes which my dad always declared as take-out food- *take out to the dog*! 4-H was my life savior. The cooking projects, the crafts, the wellness programs were all enlightening and applicable to life. I actually ended up as a 4-H leader teaching the projects when I was in my mid 20's.

One class we were holding in the Community hall when boom-crash down went one of those huge dangling lights. Lucky it did not hurt anyone. The day of achievement when we presented our creations for them to be judged, was exciting. The accompanying note book had to be just so or you didn't get your plaque and the symbolic spoon. That was another collection to add to my existing postcard, stamp, rock, and royalty pics collections. I was a collector and still am.

After 4-H, it was common to join Junior Farmers. That was a great forum to meet folks from across the province. It involved lots of fundraising initiatives like dances, recipe books, and dairy booths. By summer's end, you knew how to make milkshakes! For each club within the county, there seemed to be a cookbook of local folk's favorite recipes. Mine is so stained and still used. I treasure seeing whose recipe it is.

We then refer to the cookies as Virginia's choc chip cookies; Trinkie's jellied Christmas salad, or Bev's cheese cake. Mine were the best- just sayin'.

Of course many also met their life partners at one of the Junior Farmer events or another. I recall Ken who whistled while he danced. He was an awesome square dancer and round dancer. I should have connected more with him. Perhaps life would have been significantly different.

As the saying goes, "Sittin' and wishin' won't change my fate. The Lord provides the fishin' but I have to dig the bait"

CHAPTER TWELVE

My brother got off with a lot of things, not just because he was the baby but also because he was a boy. He knew it and maximized it. As a family we received many boxes of chocolates for Christmas. My mom would hide boxes among the clothes in our room. Of course we sneaked chocolates. When Easter came there would only be few chocolates left. With me having rotten teeth, I got the blame. To this day I am the diabetic and he can eat sweets hand over fist. Gosh that irked me. Just in case you are questioning quantities, I could only eat a few. I never have had a sweet tooth. I preferred the chocolates with the nuts. That holds true to this day!

My younger brother would kick me under the kitchen table. I'd kick back. Except one time, I missed and lam-based my dad. That did not have such a good ending. Allan would throw peas across the table at me and never get caught nor ever reprimanded. You know who was always identified as the culprit.

It is what it is.

The meals were silent. No radio was allowed unless it was 12:30 obituaries on CJET in Smiths Falls. There was a Saturday morning auctioneer on that we listened too if my dad was not in the house. My mom always said they were going to auction me off. I was petrified and listened for my name. Thankfully it never was announced.

In speaking of being told things: my mom told us the whipper-poor-will would get us if we weren't in bed on time. It wasn't until her senior years my brother confessed to her how traumatized we were. We believed her, hook, line and sinker!

As a kid I was not allowed to be baking. My dad hated that. Once he came in when my hands were in the flour. Talk about messages askew. He said, "Get her out of that or I'll split your head open and put her back in where she came from." I was befuddled- I don't think I came from her head, plus I was dreadfully scared just from his tone alone, that he'd actually do it.

My mom never told me about the menstrual cycle- just handed me some books that explained how to use the pads and a belt. I guess that constituted the birds and bees talk as well. I simply wrote sanitary pads on the grocery list and she writes in her journal-"Maria must have started her periods recently." Her diary was a scribbler left on the dresser by the pot. No-no not the pot you smoke, but the inside commode which had to be emptied daily. At nighttime the outhouse was too far, too cold and you would wake up the household looking for a flashlight, so inside was more convenient. Standard joke was the rich had a canopy over the bed; the rest of us had a "can of pee" under the bed!!!!

Historically the poor sold their urine for tanning hides. When you were "piss poor," that is what you did to survive- you sold your piss to the tannery for money. We never did that.

With no one to neither guide nor explain anything to me in childhood, I listened, assumed, and conscientiously took the path of least notice, the least anguish, and the least fear. I was blessed with lots of avenues for activity on the family farm so I didn't stew as much as I would have if I had been idle. I naively motored on through school classes, gym etc. Nothing slowed me down, not even my menstrual cycle, which seemed to limit activities of other girls.

Interesting the assaults never occurred during my periods. But I was late in starting my periods so perhaps that played a role. I was like fifteen or so. I was a late bloomer. It was God's way of protecting me from pregnancy perhaps.

To this day, siblings will deny my experiences to the point of labelling me delusional. They were not in my shoes so how can their version trump mine? That form of denial is just to protect themselves from accountability and acceptance. If you accept ownership or acknowledgement, you are then sub-consciously designed to take corrective action. How do you console when you aren't demonstrative? Whatever it is in life, once you admit, you are naturally designed to bring change. Denial keeps one stagnant. That's my bio family!

Even in writing this book, I know there will be heavy resentment and possible retaliation. My version will be deemed erroneous and myself painted as a black sheep. I know what I experienced. I am mentally cognizant!

It is what it is.

CHAPTER THIRTEEN

Much of my childhood remains a mystery while parts took shape with plausible explanations as I grew, and underwent counselling as an adult. My heart still grieves for the injustices and improprieties that were overlooked or negated. Am I damaged for life? It feels like no-one will love me as I am. I give up on relationships with a man. I am broken.

In grade eight a fellow student was shot to death as well as his sister, by his father. He sat across from me in class. I liked him. There were no counselling or support services for us. My Dad had guns. My Dad had anger. I felt he didn't care about me... Already afraid of my Dad, this magnified my apprehension. Was I safe? I'm still scared of guns. I still don't know what happened as to why? Where was the mom? It affected me greatly

Later years, my dear friend and his three brothers died in a fire. We had been at a Hallowe'en dance till closing time. That was the night the clocks turned back. Apparently they had put some oil on the stove to make French fries, fell asleep and the fire ignited. The smoke killed them. The time was obscure. It was so hard to believe, let alone accept.

Definitely as a teen I was diagnosed as an "emotional" child. I flew under the radar. If anyone knew of my struggles they did not want to interject. And function I did- no thanks to supports, for they were unknown. I am a perfectionist at painting on a smile and quick to distract with a sense of humor. I only had God. God was the person I prayed to for safety. Safety I never seemingly received although folks will say He kept you alive. Perhaps God was simply the person I cried to- *Help me, save me, protect me, and change the circumstances*". Unanswered prayers it seemed. Yet I did not question the existence of God.

My parents observed Sunday as a day of rest. Basic chores and nothing else other than visiting was done. My Mom and we kids went to church after my oldest brother got married. He lived next door to us. We walked down to his house and piled in the car with his family. It was fun to get dressed up including wearing a hat.

My Dad never wanted to go to heaven simply because he didn't want to fly around playing a harp all day. How could the alternative of hell be more appealing? See neither rhyme nor reason to things, existed in my family.

People believe everyone goes to heaven. That is not scripturally correct. God gave us a choice. Accept Christ and be saved for eternity or reject the Lord and you will be condemned for all eternity. *It is not of works lest any man should boast.*(Romans-The Bible)

Although we were not classified as a religious or spiritual family, we were still not allowed to do much on the day of rest. Could it be because Grandpa was a Baptist minister that we adhered to such observances? In reference to the quietness of Sundays, in my infinite wisdom I thought I could do my embroidery project below table level and would be undetected. Drats!!! I stitched everything to my pants!!!

Like clockwork there always was a pot of pork hock soup for Sunday supper in the cooler/cold months. Yuck!!!!

Apparently through the depression years, they ate so much pasta my Dad hated it. I on the other hand deem pasta as my comfort food. My dad would eat the spaghetti sauce by the bowlful. We'd have pasta when my dad was off at fall thrashings.

I hated pork and still detest it. I was only small, when my dad had butchered a pig. He then hung it in a tree to cure. He needed a board to keep the legs apart. So he asked me to hold the legs apart. My arms were up higher than my head spreading this huge body of meat apart. My arms grew tired: my grip slipped off the legs. My head was trapped inside the body of a dead pig. YUCK!!!!!. I hated the smell. Of course I got in trouble for non-compliance. The job was too big for me and negative consequences reigned. If I was a boy… blah…blah…blah.

My oldest brother was a hoot in many ways. He swore he could tell pumpkin pie from squash pie. One Thanksgiving he devoured the best pumpkin pie ever, so he claims. It was squash pie. One can use squash to substitute for pumpkin with no recipe changes.

I always screened his girlfriends. His existing wife of fifty-five years bribed me with costume jewellery! That's what I tell her. She really is a gem. I would sit between him and his dates. They would give me a lecture when he wasn't around. I'd tell him. They would be dumped!!! Now he would have me scratch his back in return for ballet lessons. The lessons never happened but I did learn to be a pimple popper!

Although I slept with mom, she never made any effort to console, identify or alleviate my tears. Strange. Mom never hugged me nor stroked my back when I lay crying in the bed. Come to think of it, I never heard her laugh. I think she was quite devoid of emotion. Although I did see some tears at her sister's funeral. Perhaps she was burnt out after eight kids, a troublesome husband, rural isolation and trapped by poverty.

Reflecting on caring and expressions of affection, I do recall a time where I fell down the stairs when a syrup customer was at the house. Was crying and shocked when Harry said "for God's sake man, pick the child up." I got to sit on my Dad's knee!

Interestingly I had a psychiatrist who said it was a wonder I wasn't a prostitute or into drugs given my upbringing. I believe God held me together.

My mom was always knitting socks or mitts during the cooler months. She could knit and read at the same time. We knew it was mitts for birthdays and Christmas but never quite sure what color. My brother and I had to help her take a skein and turn it into a ball of yarn. We would get inside and spin around and around and around until the task was done. Our gifts were fundamentally functional items.

Christmas was brightened by parcels from my aunt. She sent the most novel things. A great joy was when the general store in Brooke called. An uncle had left a parcel for us. There would be two bottles of ginger ale, a bag of hard candies, chocolate covered cookies, a bag of mixed nuts and I'm not sure of what else. Oh the joy!!

One year there was this particular doll I wanted so badly. I had been in the Beamish store when I fell in love. I even kissed it goodbye. I was so taken by it. Somehow my mom purchased it for me. My mom didn't know I knew she had hidden it in a suitcase. Every morning when I got up I kissed that doll and hid it again. I was so ecstatic that I got it. That is until my niece who liked to emulate me, got one the same after Christmas. Why couldn't I be an individual?

The Christmas tree was real and only came into the house the day before Christmas. It went out the day before New Year's. With a wood stove and only one room it was a danger. It would ignite very fast as it dried out, even though we watered it copiously. One time while I watched my mom stuff the turkey, I was rocking backwards in the rocking chair when wallop- I went backwards into that tree. OUCH!!!

We raised turkeys for Christmas sales. They were forever getting out of the pen and roosting in the trees. Never argue with a tom turkey!!!! Gosh how I hated the day they butchered. Turkey's everywhere!!! Thank God I was at school while they did the deed.

My sister was like clockwork always giving my brother a Hardy Boys book and I got Cherry Ames or Nancy Drew. One year she made me baby doll pj's. I quickly wrapped it back up thinking it was for one of my younger nieces. Overall the excitement outweighed what other kids got as gifts. It was a while before we returned to school so the comparison of gifts was easy to disregard with a simple explanation of "I forget."

Mother Teresa said the most terrible poverty was/is to feel unloved and unwanted. That was me and still resonates with me. Loneliness verses freedom, is also a point of interpretation and questions. Aloneness differs from loneliness. I am free to do as I choose but I do feel intense loneliness. When going somewhere I say there are three of us- me, myself and I. We concur and everything is grand. Some restaurants ask if we all want menus and I assure them, we can share!

Was I just plain neglected as a child? Or maybe just not important enough for anyone to really care?...

Maslow (1943, 1954) developed a five stage pyramid of hierarchy needs for one to mature into self-actualization. I think I am an example of his theory.

If these needs are not satisfied the human body cannot function optimally. Maslow considered physiological needs the most important as all the other needs become secondary until these needs are met.

1. Biological and physiological needs - air, food, drink, shelter, warmth, sex, sleep, etc.

2. Safety needs - Once an individual's physiological needs are satisfied, the needs for security and safety become salient. People want to experience order, predictability and control in their lives. These needs can be fulfilled by the family and society (e.g. police, schools, business and medical care).

For example, emotional security, financial security (e.g. employment, social welfare), law and order, freedom from fear social stability, property, health and wellbeing (e.g. safety against accidents and injury).

3. Love and belongingness needs - after physiological and safety needs have been fulfilled; the third level of human needs is social and involves feelings of belongingness. The need for interpersonal relationships motivates behavior

Examples include friendship, intimacy, trust, and acceptance, receiving and giving affection and love. Affiliating, being part of a group (family, friends, work).

4. Esteem needs are the fourth level in Maslow's hierarchy - which Maslow classified into two categories: (i) esteem for oneself (dignity, achievement, mastery, independence) and (ii) the desire for reputation or respect from others (e.g., status, prestige).

Maslow indicated that the need for respect or reputation is most important for children and adolescents and precedes real self-esteem or dignity.

5. Self-actualization needs are the highest level in Maslow's hierarchy, and refer to the realization of a person's potential, self-fulfillment, seeking personal growth and peak experiences. Maslow (1943) describes this level as the desire to accomplish everything that one can, to become the most that one can be.

It is not so difficult to identify where I was fluctuating throughout my life. No wonder I am who I am.

CHAPTER FOURTEEN

Not so sure if any older siblings got attention either, although the older ones have mighty different recollections of their life as a youngster. They recalled my parents going to dances together, school concerts in the cutter, sleigh rides and so on. Never knew my parents to dance until after my dad passed at age 96. I had remarked to an elder sister how at Good Companion's Senior's dance, I saw a man who resembled my dad, if only he had danced. Apparently they used to go all the time on Sat nights with my oldest sibling and her husband. My mom would often step dance at home to jigs. I loved old fashion square dancing but this modern stuff leaves me as a viewer only.

I recall going to an Agricultural dance where the band was playing. A school friend more like acquaintance asked me to dance and to my refusal of not knowing how, Sheri, simply instructed me to wiggle your arms and legs and butt. So that's what I did and do. I am enthralled with ballroom dancing but can't find the left foot verses right foot! I'm tone deaf and can't pick up a rhythm if I tried, and yes, I have tried. Now seeing the grandkids move their bodies to Tik-Tok befuddles me. I didn't know body parts could twist, or gyrate into such contortions!

I was very fortunate to be chosen as a 4-H chaperone for an exchange with Alberta 4-H members. My co-host remains my friend today. Ironically they raised sheep by the hundreds. Taking in the Calgary Stampede was exciting and exhausting. When the exchange came to Eastern Ontario, we lost an Alberta kid in the area of the Parliament Buildings in Ottawa. Because I was familiar with Ottawa I was elected to wait behind to scout for him. Somehow he managed to get himself over to the Museum of Science which was our next stop. I met up there with them. I was frantic- how do you tell a parent I lost their child???? At the end of both exchange dates, the proper kids were returned to their respective homes. Just in case we did lose someone we checked and double checked. What a great experience!

I also benefitted from being selected in 4-H to go to leadership conferences. Unfortunately being co-captain of the Blue team at Guelph ended in sad terms. My poor cousin Arthur was electrocuted on the job at age 16. Poor lad never stood a chance when the construction company gave him a three prong drill with two pronged electrical cord. His glasses were found many feet away from his body. His boots were blown right off his body! A former Agricultural Rep was travelling to Perth from Guelph so offered me a ride. Running out of gas on the 401 in Toronto was not his plan, but it happened. Left sitting in the car, I was so scared. I arrived home in time for the funeral- such a sad day. To be frank about it- it sucked.

The conference was great but all the experiences were not. The Cattleman's Association was also meeting in Guelph so my oldest brother was there as well as some other county men. One came to my bedroom just as I was ready to crawl into bed. I aborted his attempts to fondle me and thanks to my brother arriving, I was saved from further activity. The two left together. Did my brother suspect anything? That man was a married man!!! My brother never commented. My other 4-H leader was accused of sodomizing his kids, my mom inquired if he ever touched me but she never inquired about anything else. He didn't, but his brother-in-law in Guelph commented to me on how my sister was an easier target than me. What?

My brother, the 4-H agricultural leader was the recipient of a book after my essay on his leadership skills, was selected as the winning essay entry. He always gave me the hardest time. He never clued me in when the Rep was coming to inspect our calves. Mind you as 4-H members we implemented a phone chain to advise others to be prepared for the visit. Same system adults used to inform of Jehovah Witnesses or ministers on the prowl, worked for us teens!

My brother never wanted to be accused of favoritism, so any accolades were achieved through my own hard work and merit. Now for showmanship, you had to keep your eye on the judge. Frig... I walked straight into his car because both eyes were on the judge! Trading calves was a gamble. Doug kept oats in his pocket to lead his calf so when we traded; I had a free for all on my hands! A friend Ernie, came out to see how to show as he was showing his dairy calf in his local fair the following week. My calf pulled a great stunt that year at the fair. The calf was awarded first place, and rather than going to the spot, simply laid down- not to be moved at any measure! Talk about embarrassing!!! The judge simply lined the other calves beside her!!!

I was so attached to my calves, naming them and usually they went on to be a heifer in my dad's herd. My final year of high school, it was implied that my calf would go to the sales barn. Every night after school, I'd walk in the laneway, drop by the barn to see my calf, as the barn was before the house and horrors of horrors, my calf's stall was empty. Rushing to the house, frantic, I was told the calf went to market!! I was devastated. I didn't even get to say goodbye. Yes I was emotional! For one whole year I refused to eat any beef anywhere, any shape, any form, in case it was my calf.

Now my brother's calf was also sold and he got the money but I didn't. You see girls are not important was not only vocalized but practises reinforced the message. I was not important.

Academically I achieved well in high school. I won the science award and the math recipient, Brian wanted to switch trophies - no way with my math skills or rather my lack of skills.

If you attended class the day before exams, most of the teachers indicated what were to be the exam questions. For math, this entailed nearly a page of mathematical operations to get the answer. No calculators back then. Often I had no idea of those operations, but memorized the final answer. A particular question befuddled me so I simply wrote a mix of operations followed by the right answer. The teacher remarked that I must have gotten confused transcribing from the scrap paper to the exam so I only lost one point! I had no idea of how to solve the equation!!!

For a particular Commencement, my Dad drove me up to the high school but wouldn't come in. My older sister had driven my Mom and her fair entries to the fairgrounds. I received so many trophies, the principal asked a family member to come forward to help me. I nearly died of embarrassment as I had no-one present. Thankfully a neighbor lady came forward, hugged me and whispered, "Are you here alone?" As soon as I could escape the congratulatory greetings, I escaped out to the truck. It was humiliation to the toes and back again. Why????

There is a small black trunk in the attic above the garage with the proof of my achievements. Every year, I was top of my class. Now mind you, I did all my homework by coal oil lamp. No electricity. Maple syrup served as glue for projects. Today my kids and grandkids, laugh at my sports trophies when they contemplate my obese size now.

It is what it is.

CHAPTER FIFTEEN

When I went to post-secondary school, I paid everything myself. My brother had his money from selling his calf for tuition. It is not that I am envious of my brother; I am simply stating how things were. Well maybe I was/am envious and resentful. Although I had student loans, I was able to secure a job. I worked as a waitress one block south of Bloor and Yonge in Toronto, to pay for my schooling and housing costs, plus food was free for me at the restaurant.

I have to give my mom credit for accompanying me to the big city during a transit/subway strike. We walked many blocks to my accommodations carrying my "stuff". Perhaps due to a lack of money, we did not use a taxi. It seems it would have been easier. But then taxis were foreign to us country bumpkins.

At the recommendation of my sister I connected with some of her friends from where she lived. I agreed to go to a Halloween house party with this chap. He would then drive me to the bus stop to return back to my parents place for the weekend. Damn animal- he tried to feel me up when we went to get the coats to leave. He had me pinned on the bed when another guest interrupts asking what he thought he was doing.

At that time I also found out at that time my boyfriend was two-timing me. I wondered why he did not maintain regular contact but discovered through his uncle he was seeing someone else. I'll never forget the night he and I watched

Alfred Hitchcock's movie _**The Birds**_ before driving home. This huge owl dipped down in front of us and I screamed. I still tense when I see the huge flocks of blackbirds, seagulls, or crows.

Of course there was the time we rode the pair of work horses bareback from one village through the back gravel roads to his father's farm. It must have been a good 25 miles. Just as we got to the farm a car spooked my horse. Off I went. Monday I couldn't go to school because I couldn't walk. Never repeated that act again. Overall, I had good memories of him. RIP Rick.

My first landlady In Toronto was a bird of a different feather. I had been home for break, been sick with bronchitis and didn't return to school for a week. We had curfews. I phoned letting her know I was catching the midnight bus back to Toronto and would be arriving early in the morning. It was so cold, and the subway was not yet open so this taxi driver gave me a free ride to the house. He told me the area was not safe at that hour. Little did I know. That landlady bat kept the door chains on and would not let the other two girls let me in. She was on the school's recommended housing list. The school director took her off immediately after hearing what she did.

I moved out of there to a dear elderly lady's home on Glen Forest Road, further from school but who was incredible gracious. I did her errands in return for companionship and accommodation. One morning, I took the subway the wrong direction so I was racing against time to get to English class. Shooting up the stairs at St. Claire station I bump into my old English teacher. As if!!! Needless to say I was always late to his classin high school as well.

One evening at this restaurant where I worked on weekends and after school, this chap goes straight in behind the counter to open the cash drawer and is counting the money. Not thinking, or rather thinking of protecting the restaurant, I marched up to him briskly inquiring his business. Turned out he was the accountant. Boss Chris asked what if he had a gun- shrugging I retorted-"I supposed I'd be dead"!!!

Chris arranged for this male relative or friend, to cover for him by closing the restaurant this particular weekend, and told him to be sure to give me a ride home in his absence. That man closed up the restaurant on time, and proceeded to set up porno movies. I never saw that before. He then wanted me to engage in strange sex acts. I threatened I'd tell. I booted it out of there and took the subway home which was scary at that time of night. Should have taken a taxi!

Another young man came in for his usual cup of coffee so I invite him to enjoy the hockey game on the telly at the back with the men. He refuses but wants to ask questions.

"Were you out of the country this summer?
Where you down south?
Did you take an order for 500 pigs' feet?"

At this point I am flabbergasted how does he know about this? I turn 500 shades of red and he says it was you that went Oink. Oink, Oink?" With no intercom system, I had to shout down to Walter and with the accents, I needed to clarify that my interpretation of the order was accurate.

The accents were so strong I had problems deciphering the conversation. I never had an order like that before!

I stood out as a white person in a sea of brown. This man took note of me and recalled me in Toronto!!!! What a chance meeting. To me it proved one should always be on their best behavior for you never know when it will catch up to you!

I met the High Commissioner for Canada at the Canada Day and was shocked he knew where I was really from. In fact, he had my older school colleague build his cottage for him 1.5 hours west of Ottawa. I went to school with his carpenter!

That trip was quite the endeavor for this country bumpkin: first time for many, many things. A third world country is a learning experience. I spent an afternoon playing soccer with my nephew and he tells everyone at dinner we played football. Now the ball is in the boot!

On a trip to the interior on the mail plane I still maintain the pilot was lost when we flew helter skelter. I was holding the map for him while we bounced around in a thunderstorm!! Here we are above the jungle and he knows where he's going? We did reach the destination. I loved being in the sky so high.

Grown men had to strip before flying out of the interior. That was a sight for young eyes! There was a chance they were smuggling diamonds. The guava bread was baking on the roof of their huts. When Grandad gave me snake as a snack the first night I had two snacks- one going down- one coming up! It was quite granular and spicy. Ew-w-w

Returning home on commercial flight, there was a layover on one of the islands. This chap joined me at the table for supper and immediately thought it was an invitation to share my bed! What is it with men??? I'm not even in the category of attractive. I'm a plain Jane with a flat bosom.

Several years ago, I made a long distance call to check up on my mother. She had broken her knee cap in the Toronto Pearson Airport so was in this third world country recuperating. I had never made an overseas call before. Fifteen minutes of jibber-jabber about the weather, Christmas, etc. before I realized I was connected to the wrong country. I had the right name but Bell hooked me up wrong. That poor lady was so hesitant when I asked how mom was. She replied, "Mom's dead!" WHAT! I was speechless. Why did no one tell me?

Bell was good enough to erase the cost and acknowledge their mistake.

It is what it is!

Living in the city was a new experience and I learned. On the way home from a babysitting job, the mom asked "turn left?", to which I said "right". She turned right. Now I say, "correct." That was a valuable life lesson. Another set of parent's had their child asleep when I arrived. They lived in this tall house with a different floor for each of the kitchen, living, room, bathroom, and bedrooms. What a task to find the child!!!

How I wonder what transpired in the lives of these youngsters? Where are they today?

CHAPTER SIXTEEN

Mind you there were a number of other snags between my birth and today. Overall I survived the battles with scars and gained an understanding for others experiencing similar situations. Again my safe ports seemed to be unknown.

In my role as a Social Service Worker I had so many people tell me that it was like I really understood them. My life experiences may not have been foreign to some but why I had to experience so many trial and tribulations often overwhelms me. Logically I really didn't need all the experiences to be successful professionally! It has been and will continue to be an argument that text book learning does not match experience. We all can't have experience in all things and yet we as professionals in any field, need to recognize we can be in over our heads.

It is similar to a know-it-all. As much as they have extensive knowledge they fail to recognize they do not know it all.

Scripturally the Lord tells us to remove the speck from our own eye before attempting to remove it from someone else's eye. Well I have the brown speck in my eye. In public school when horsing around with another lad, he threw a burr from the burdock plant at me. It accidently went into my eye. The doctor could not see it, so sent me home. It bothered me all night so back to the doctor's I went. Fortunately my brother could see it and he pulled it out. It scarred my eye. I use it as a demonstration to others. The tiniest thing can leave a mark. Your tiniest actions will leave a mark- good or bad.

I called a Crisis line once for support during a time of feeling overwhelmed. Yes I told them I just had a ganglion cyst removed off my foot therefore a lot of pain plus that my partner had recently passed. The counsellor suggested I walk, or get my partner to drive me to the corner store, which was 10 km away. Yep I'll get right on that!!!

Another counsellor on a Crisis line at a different time suggested I identify things I liked AFTER I told her I found myself suicidal with NO interests. Hello-o-o anyone listening??? I was feeling so down, so wanting to die, so overwhelmed by everything. I hung up and called the Distress line for support.

Truly some folks in the helping professions are fence turtles. A fence turtle is a turtle that some person put on a fence post. It had no ability to get there by itself. We have a lot of politicians that are fence turtles!!!!!

Talking about confidentiality among those in the Social Worker field, you always need to be mindful of what you say. As a child I heard this trapper friend of my dad's speak of this young Social Worker in her short mini-skirt and tiny car coming to investigate the well-being of his kids. He went out with his gun to meet her. Years later, like a good thirty one years later, one of my preceptor's at college talked of her young friend who went out to investigate this hillbilly family in her mini skirt, small car and how this burly guy came out with his gun. She mentioned the county but no names. I knew who she was speaking off!!! Confidentiality is a must and so innocently broken by a slip of the tongue.

It is what it is.

When my clients or friends talked of affection shown by parents, aunts, uncles and grandparents, I could only envy. You see jealous is when you had something and lost it but envy was when you never had the experience/item that you so desire. Young kids are jealous when a new one arrives. They have lost the attention and time they once had. I have no recollection of affection from either parent except for that one time of sitting on my dad's knee. I never knew grandparents. They were deceased before I was born.

I met this lovely, dear old lady living not far from me. She was the epitome of a Grandma. Within a couple of visits, I was so comfortable with her; I told her that she was so special to me. If I could choose a Grandma, she'd be my choice. She declared right there and then I was her granddaughter! I was adopted by her. I lavished her with so much love, and she me, fulfilling my adult need for a Grandma.

I often visited her in the nursing home and once upon leaving said-"well, my friend, I need to get motoring." My gosh, she nearly jumped off the bed as she wagged her finger at me, admonishing me- "I am not your friend. I am your grandmother!!!" Whoa!... I had been told.

This is borrowed from an unknown author on Facebook, but is for you Gran:

"Wanted to call you today to say I love you, but your old number is no longer in service. I tried the operator, she said I'm sorry, I have no number for you. I tried to go to your house, but you don't live there anymore. The post office has no forwarding address. I guess heaven is just too far away. I love you, I miss you. You are in my heart always. Loved ones gone but not forgotten".

It is what it is! RIP GRAN

Now I was so fortunate to meet another young lady that I often call my adopted daughter. She was in the waiting room of the local hospital when I was there. The intercom malfunctioned, leaving the nurse repeatedly saying-"Hello-do you need to see a doctor?" We all collectively would answer "yes we do!" Samure has such an infectious laugh. She was in covered in poisonous parsnip but still could laugh. How I love that laugh. She had recently colored her hair various colors like green, blue, pink and so on. I called her dad and asked, "Had he had sex with a peacock or parrot?" He gingerly asks "why?" so I said, "look at the hair Samure has!!!"

So if she is my daughter, and he is her dad, and her granny is my granny, who is tracking this genealogical connection?

It is what it is.

Naturally if something could happen, it would happen to me. I attended a mom and tots group where we learned to make grapevine wreaths. All excited and gung ho, I set off with the boys to pick grapevines. Well, my oh my, by evening my hands had swelled up, and my face was so swollen I couldn't see to do anything. Come to learn I had picked poison ivy vines!! I didn't even know they came in vines. Day after day I had to go to the hospital to be checked. Thank goodness my mom came to help me out. I got the poison ivy cleared up when I come down with shingles. Now that is PAIN!! I had my shirt rolled up so my belly was not touching anything. It was so very, very uncomfortable. The doctor believed I, in a weaken state had been exposed to chicken pox in one of the trips to the hospital. Cautiously I ask if my kids would then get chicken pox from my shingles seeing it is the same herpes zoster virus. No,.. he doubted it. One morning Chris gets up… covered in spots,… then Simone and several hours later I see George blistering. I phone the doctor in tears," you said…." Well, consolation was that we were all ill together. Thank goodness for my neighbor who helped out so much. My hubby was not compassionate or helpful at all. He might as well have been on Mars. As long as he had his alcohol and meals, he was content.

When it comes to overall health, aging has brought many challenges. Besides osteoarthritis, diabetes, fibromyalgia, obesity, and mental a health issues, I have an Essential Tremor. The doc regularly assesses that it is not Parkinson's but no- it is Essential Tremor. That basically means I shake, especially my hands. Sometimes trying to consume food is nothing short of a mess. I wear more than I eat. It is genetic but I do not know any other family history of it. I can no longer hold my hands to sew or knit, paint or exercise any fine motor skills. Even my writing is affected. Some days are better than others. This is basically a brain malfunction. Some medication helps but ultimately is a challenge to manage. Don't be surprised if you see me drink my coffee with a straw. Apparently a good stiff drink would help…

It is what it is.

CHAPTER SEVENTEEN

Times at home growing up, were rough but thankfully my dear neighbor, who unfortunately, just passed recently at 99 years of age, always encouraged me in all my endeavors-cooking, track and field,-sewing. That famial induced embarrassment of myself continued into my early adult life. In fact, it may still be there. It is.

I was use to entering the local fair to win money to buy things- you know just things you want! Without further contemplation I just naturally entered in the local fair after I was married. My then husband was so embarrassed that we couldn't even go to see if I had won any prizes. It was not until his best friend's wife called to say I won a lot of prizes did he consent for us, not him, to go to the fair to see the results on the following day. I had won so many ribbons. In fact I was the top new exhibitor.

The kids also entered as they grew up- almost a rite of passage. That was always a solo job getting the entries to town and to round up those entries at the conclusion of the fair. Just remembering the embarrassment he imposed makes my face still burn from humiliation. I know I can bake and cook, but the constant negativity destroyed me. Yet through it all, I got to know many people and the kids had spending money.

It is what it is.

Now being a single parent of four, who often had friends over, often it would become confusing. In fact I made a trip to Morrisburg to pick up Simone's friend, I asked Chris to take Daniel to the bathroom while I ran into the grocery store for ice cream. I return to the car and counted seven heads so off I drove. Ten miles down the road I realize Daniel's friend is serious when he says Daniel is not in the car. I thought they were pranking me. Goodness me.... I left the wee fellow back at the parking lot! I should have had eight heads since I picked up one more! Gravy... how could this have happened!!! Swiftly I turn around and boot it back. There he is calmly sitting on the bench swinging his legs. Later I ask, "What would you have done if I didn't return?" Oh- he had decided he would walk home (40 km). Do you know who had nightmares that night? Nope, not him. I had a terrible night!!!!

That had reminded me of running the daycare centre in Ottawa. A certain child came every second Friday. This particular Friday his dad comes in and I freeze on the spot. For the life of me I can't recall seeing that child. I must have gone white, and dad played it out- 'Oh I came early to pick up....' I frantically thinking, scared I'd lost a child, breathed such a sigh of relief when he says he came to get the sweater. Whew!!!!

My memory fails me on a regular basis and more so as I age. I go to the dentist for my schedule cleaning. I can't recall what I had for breakfast but I tell the dentist, I feel like I'm teething. 65 and I think I am teething? X-rays are done and sure enough there is a big tooth on the screen. That tooth was not there two years ago. Worse still it had a cavity present! I'm thinking, I AM truly rotten to the core. He makes arrangements to pull out this impacted eye tooth.

How dare he call it the tooth- that is WALDO. We don't know where he came from but Waldo was messing with my sinus cavity. When I had a tube inserted for a blocked eye duct, that surgeon could feel a bony blockage, was it Waldo moving down? But still, where did he come from???

Now interestingly enough, my youngest child has a full set of teeth that has not descended. I know the tooth fairy made regular visits so yes his baby teeth came out. He elected to let it be. There was no guarantee the additional set would drop down if the existing set was pulled. 20 years later, he has had no dental issues. Sometimes we have to let things just be as they are.

It is what it is.

CHAPTER EIGHTEEN

After Toronto, I went to Carleton University for one year. That was quite interesting. Academically I did well. The philosophy department wanted me to major in philosophy. I still don't know how the grass is green, pigs fly and therefore the sky is blue????? My thesis was on the rational and irrational behaviors of mankind against mankind. This was before 9:11. Just think how I could expand on that now.

Doing laundry, I inadvertently dumped my textbook in the washer- whoops. This was while I was coaching another chap how to separate darks from lights while doing his laundry! Remember I was not raised on electronics so all this power stuff was foreign to me. My experience was the wringer washer with gas motor and a clothesline.

I befriended a young lady, Holly, who did Children's TV shows. She needed to bake a cake and knew I had done 4-H so I was to be the guiding force. We laughed so much as she took on the task. We had flour from ceiling to floor. The cake was delicious.

I lived close to the university in a house owned by a professor. Struggling to meet a deadline, he came up at 2 a.m. to ask me to refrain from typing. Yes the old typewriter was one where it went ping, ping, ping. Sound travelled between the floors. I took a break for 3 hours then one fingered typed and met the deadline.

Surprisingly, I connected with a chap that I had attempted square dancing with at the local fair. The square fell apart but we two-stepped around the dance floor. He would offer me rides home on weekends. Then the next time I ran across him was when I was in labor for my second child. He was now a doctor. We concurred he was NOT going to deliver MY child! LOL

I also met the most wonderful chap ever. We talked in depth of spiritual issues, went skating on the canal, had dinner out and in, plus shared class notes. A lady friend of his did not like me for being his friend! She always dressed in black. Gothic was in style before its time. I could not figure that out. I think that was jealousy on her part! Ironically he said he saw me with a number of kids rather than a working professional. How right he was. Unfortunately he had cancer. Petrovic- I miss you!

When it comes to religious versus spiritually, people generally have no clue how to differentiate. Religious is when you practice the rituals for a particular belief. The ritual can be the repetition of a behavior with a lack of substance to understand the behavior.-i.e. crossing one self, going to church or simply saying grace.

Spirituality has three levels-individual spirituality, community spirituality and cosmic spirituality.

*Individuality spiritu*ality is about your inner feelings of being a "good" person or a "bad" person. That resonates around positive and negative affirmations. It develops as we grow and develop. Hardship during our formative years usually develops low self-esteem or a heavy dose of resiliency. Despite the low self-esteem, I have been resilient.

The *community spirituality* has been underdeveloped. Society has kept people so busy, they neglect giving back to the community. Society is in such a chronic state that schools had to mandate 40 hours of volunteer work before a student graduates to develop community spirituality. This community spirituality shines around Christmas time as we support Toy Mountain, Salvation Army kettles and giving of gifts. I remain community oriented. It is a joy to help out where I can, when I can and however I can.

Cosmic spirituality is who or what you think is in overall control of the universe. For me it is God. The God who sent his son to die on the cross so I can go to heaven for eternity. For those of a more scientific mode, then their obligation is to keep their body as healthy as possible so there is no contamination when you return to the ground via cremation of burial.

Wavering in any of the three levels, results in an unsettled human being. Addicts are devoid of spirituality. They use substances or sex to fill up that hole. Where are you?

It is what it is.

Being on the spiritual-pastoral team at the local hospital proved to be such a wonderful experience. The data system was not set up to be the most current, so it was common to waltz into a man's room expecting a woman. Some jokesters would direct me to look under the bed!! Once I inadvertently brought the shame upon myself. Regular volunteers wore blue vests, so when our visiting guest asked what we wore I said, "Nothing!" Quickly I clarified I meant just our standard street attire!

Others were so inspirational. I had one chap who was just given a two week window of life left due to cancer. The nurse was about to give him his bath when she figured my role took precedence. He confessed his belief in Christ that day! He entered eternity soon after into the waiting arms of Jesus.

Another chap always arrogant against organized religion was tossing in turmoil when the family asked for me to visit him. Basically he and I had met in the community setting prior and he had denounced any faith in God. So when I went to see him, I was in left field as to how I could help him. He had throat cancer and was basically verbally non-responsive. I asked him a series of questions-are you worried about your wife after you pass- he shakes his head, worried about your sons, each by name- No, worried about the farm-No. I'm stuck- then I ask are you afraid to meet God- yup-well then it meant simply explaining the plan of salvation. I asked him do you believe Jesus died on the cross for you to go to heaven, he nodded yes. With my own eyes I saw that man, fold his hands in prayer formation, become at peace and died within eight hours. The family who had taken a break while I visited, could not believe the transformation.

Another dear chap, very convinced in nature evolution said he'd not conform to Christianity but would love to engage in debate with me. I was open to that. Sometimes he was asleep when I came to visit so I'd leave a note accusing him of chickening out! Well this continued for a couple of months. Finally he was in palliative care, unresponsive when I dropped by. His family said no use visiting today. They were cognizant of our debates. I said I'd say a prayer for him because by this time I knew he was seriously considering salvation. Well now- he sat up, yes sat up and said, "I believe!" lay back down, and never to speak again before he passed. WOW!

Elizabeth Kubler Ross speaks of how many reach out with their arms to those who passed prior to them. I've witnessed that many a time. You can see the outstretched arms. Someone has arrived to take them home. Some people wait for a certain person to arrive before they die, or they go when no-one is present. Patients have shared their stories of loved ones passing. Don't be afraid to talk about death. No one gets out of life alive. It is a part of the journey of living. Seems women have taken a more active step in spiritual matters then men. Or maybe I just had more novel experiences with men. Although one family facing the loss of wife and mother had negative experiences with a church so I simply offered my availability to visit and pray. Well they sought me out and we came to an understanding that yes organized religion can fail us but God won't. Prayers were said and the family felt more at ease that this woman would go to heaven. Organized religion bothers me to this day.

Another dear chap, a retired famer had zero interest in anything other than farm life. I'd tease him he was a strange farmer. He had all makes of tractors where most farmers dealtspecifically in John Deere's, Massey Ferguson's, Ford's, Case' or Cockshutt's and so on. As he declined in health he started to ask about life after death. I shared what I believed and re-iterated like his tractors, there are many variances. He died in the knowledge God saved him.

I told him a story of three local ministers meeting in the local restaurant for coffee with each laboring their practices for prayer. The Catholic priest claiming you had to kneel and cross yourself. The Pentecostal argued no you had to raise your arms reaching up to the sky while the Presbyterian simply said to simply bow your head. An old farmer sitting across from their booth spoke up-"You guys have it all wrong-the best way to pray is when you are head first in a well".

Not of such a serious note, I had a Jehovah Witness patient who asked why I wasn't visiting her as I did with her three roommates. I explained she had not consented to visits which was typical. Jehovah Witnesses normally stay within themselves. So I agreed to simply visit. She was East Indian and found the hospital food too bland. I okayed it with staff to bring her in a hot pepper I had grown. My son loves hot peppers so this was a trial run growing them. They were so hot!!! Well she made me laugh so hard. She'd take a bite and declare, "oh-la-la-la, that is hot- but I like it." This went on for the course of her meal.

Life is made up of the little things.

Laugh when you can.

Pray often and continue on.

CHAPTER NINETEEN

I had back surgery in '94 when I was forty. I had been working as a Home Support Worker when my back gave out. Pain was in my right hip and behind the right knee. Positive I had bad varicose veins, I'd have the kids' look, only for them to report there were no visible veins. Sometimes my legs would stop working and I'd have to pull my shorts by the legs forward to get mobile. Yet I never missed a day of work.

Some of those clients were angels and so appreciative while others left me scrambling. Transference is when you transmit a connection of one person onto another person. I had a client who so resembled my ex-father-in-law. I was petrified. He turned out to be so sweet. He was so kind. He was my kind of wonderful!

The timing of appointments by the office was ludicrous. You finished one place at eleven then had to be thirty minutes away for eleven. You were always behind. Add to that traffic and weather, you evidently had a mess on your hands.

One psycho-geriatric client was sure I'd get kidney infections from wearing sandals. Took her for x-rays following a fall and her biggest concern was her hair in case she wanted copies. Obviously obsessive-compulsive in how she had jars, cans and towels lined up just so, and I did not dare touch anything. Lord be merciful if you put anything out of place. She also refused any help for housekeeping duties, but once I managed to talk her into letting me change her sheets. Damn….she pulled a gun on me. I would have kissed her ass if necessary. Turned out to be a realistic looking toy gun but.....

In reality, that woman was a legend! She had her parents and her only two sisters wiped out by Typhoid fever leaving her to be raised by unrelenting, controlling grandparents. It kept her from straying for sure. She could recall in detail the white coffins of her little sisters- oh so sad. However, she was educated well and become the Justice of the Peace in addition to Municipal administrative duties. As much as she shared riding in her hubby's side car for the motorcycle, I could not picture that! Again sadness prevailed when he was killed and she was left with five youngsters. They grew up to be independent to the point they really did not visit or connect with her in her senior years. Perhaps her stern, critical demeanor played a huge part in that alienation. When she finally got into a nursing home after a number of falls, she enjoyed socialization and with regular meals and self-care, she became more at ease. A stoic woman by all costs!

Another client, the mother of my mailman had locked herself out of the house. Having no phone, I loaded her into my car hoping to catch the mailman at my house. This is before cell phones. I let the office know she was with me and fed her lunch. Eventually we found her son. She tells folks- "the big lady took me around the world"!!!!

Another dear lady had been an army airline steward in her day, and now with dementia, she would want to race to the airport whenever she heard a plane. Those were some wild, erratic walks until the plane disappeared from sight. She had the worst time losing her dentures. They could be in the garbage, in the toilet, in the freezer, in the oven, anyplace you could dream off. Her hubby was so patient with her. He religiously took her for her weekly hair appointment. Now that is my kind of man!

Family doc recommended bed rest for my back problems. With four kids and limited money, how is that possible? Thankfully he went on holiday and the substitute doc sent me straight to Ottawa for an MRI. My spine was like a leaking hose. Predictions after the MRI were that perhaps I might have a headache that night but I should be okay until the following appointment. Oh boy, I couldn't get out of bed the next morning. Thanks to Karen who really is carin' and my kids, I was rolled to the car to hit the General Hospital. I was experiencing bladder problems so in went a catheter. Seems my bladder had been holding me hostage by reducing output yet increased the frequency of voiding! Immediate surgery was the answer.

19 days hospitalized, as I waited for them to fuse the L4 and L5 herniated discs. One nurse in her infinite wisdom thought I should be off pain pills and was quickly reprimanded by the doc the next morning as I writhed in pain. I had no sensation in my right foot because the sciatica nerve was pinched.

There was an issue of electronics disappearing on the floor, and one night, I wake up with a nurse over me unplugging my radio. I called for backup and never saw her again. Thief!!

It was quite a conflab to arrange my discharge. Required to do bedrest for 10 weeks, I couldn't have my meds within the reach of my children. Yet it was okay for my 16 year old son to give me my bath!!!!! I don't think so. Finally they ordered Home Care. The kids were troopers making meals, etc. and I figured when the homemakers were present that was their time off. Some workers thought differently!

After surgery I never walked until they discharged me two days after surgery, and I was expected to walk out of the hospital. My neighbor Laurence, had brought my Taurus Wagon and we contemplated many ways to get me in the vehicle to go back home. Eventually I got in. I looked at Laurence and said. "Can I ask something?" He gives "that look" and says, "Don't ask to go to the washroom"!!! All I wanted was a milkshake from McDonald's!! Lol Thank goodness they gave a shot of morphine for the ride home. 45 minutes later I had all I could take. Yet three steps loomed in front of me to get into the house. I was so thankful my mom had come down to help out.

Once home I was on a painkiller Leritine which they had never given me prior. Did I hallucinate!!!! My bed was downstairs and I was screaming so loud that my mom and son came running. I had the scissors and was cutting perceived fishing line off my neck, luckily I did not snip my neck. Then they get me settled and I'm screaming again that the dishwasher is eating the pattern off my dishes. Chris brings me a plate to prove me wrong but I'm adamant he took it from the cupboard. Once again they got me settled. Next day pharmacist said never take that drug again or it could kill me.

To complicate matters during this time my ex tried to take one of the steel silos. The kids and my Mom had to call the cops. Then his lovely wife called threatening to beat me up. Talk about troublesome interference when I least needed it!

The chap who rented the barn from me came in to see how I was prior to the kids starting back to school. I was convinced I had reached out with my right arm and dropped the pain pills which rolled under the bed. He and the kids dismantled the room and didn't find the meds. Being so worried about not having any, I called a neighbor to pick me up some more. Lol- the meds were sitting on the night stand beside the bed- I never touched them.

It is what it is.

During convalescence, it was strange being on the opposite side of a HSW- receiving help rather than giving. Several times when I complained about the efficiency of the staff, I was told they all weren't good workers like I was- in my mind, they should have been. We got the same pay! One lady Marlene took all four kids for back to school shopping. She returned intact. They behaved so well she treated them to ice cream!!! I am indebted to her forever.

Another HSW had the gall to gossip about me and my kids to my neighbor. She felt the kids were not helping enough. They were on duty all the time when she wasn't there!!!! I was furious and adamantly told the agency NEVER to send her back. Gossiping is against the agency policies. Insolent!!!

Following surgery I had major headaches. Once I was airlifted to the Civic campus for an air bubble in my spine that had travelled to the brain. It would have been a great helicopter ride if I had been feeling well! It was new for our local hospital to have a helicopter pad. I made the front page of the newspaper. They snapped a shot as I was being loaded in. I recognized the running shoes.

Another time Karen accompanied me to the General for a spinal tap. The doctor was young and oh so handsome. Amazing how many docs were cute!!!! Even my surgeon! This handsome hunk, sweetie, gave the tray to Karen to hold while he injected the needle. Well I screamed, like a blood curling scream, and my leg jumped. "Oh dear", he says. Apparently he had hit a nerve.

It is what it is!

Seems on several occasions, I was in so much pain, I'd beg the driver of the vehicle to let me out and run over me. After another surgery I was released from day surgery simply because the nurse's shift was over. I was vomiting profusely. That went on for 24 hours. The family doctor was none too pleased with the staff! I was dehydrated and returned to hospital. I should have never been discharged!

It is what it is.

CHAPTER TWENTY

Speaking of the kids now aged 16, 14, 12 and 10, they wanted to have Thanksgiving. Usually I hosted the family of approximately 40 family folks or went back home. This year after the back surgery, was a no go for either option. So off the oldest two go with a neighbor and a blank cheque to get the fixin's.

Directing them from my bed, I hear them arguing in the kitchen whether it is a boy or girl turkey. Daniel comes in with the neck in tongs and says "Mom this is a boy turkey right? It came out of the back end!"

Dressed to the hilt, Simone had on long rubber gloves and the other two boys sported my only two aprons! So with the dressing made, we figured we would have a lovely supper. At noon when the nurse came, she commented the turkey was sitting on the counter. They forgot to put it in the oven!!!! We had a delicious supper at eight p.m.!!!

Another time, as a single parent and frugal times, I had said we needed to trim everyone's toenails. Jokingly I said we would have toenail soup from their long nails. By golly, Chris gathered up the toenails and dumped them into my tomato soup!!!! Down the toilet, went lunch!!!

Seems the Taurus Wagon, was the centre of many escapades. I parked it by the hedge after work as usual. The keys hung on a rack inside the door. The next morning I go out on my way to work, I was sure the car was closer to the hedge than I parked it. The seat feels closer to the steering wheel. Something is amiss. I look on the ceiling; there is a small dab of the white and blueberry filling from a donut. I know someone else has driven my vehicle. Chris denies any knowledge. But wait… there is a bike leaning against the garage. It disappeared during the day!!!

Years later Simone is working as a bike carrier in the city when she runs into a former resident of the hamlet near us. He asks her if I ever figured out who took my car. He took it for a joy ride and donut run into the city!!!!!

One of the most awful, dreadful things I had to do after the separation was make a new will. While married, my sister and her husband agreed to take custody of the kids if anything should happen to us, the parents. Figuring it would be the same deal after the separation I was very taken back when I was told they no longer wanted to take on that responsibility. Wow- that hurt. Not having any other possibilities, given the paternal side were not appropriate, I had to comprise a list of requests for all four to go into CAS care. I wanted them to remain together and in a Christian home and the list went on. That tore the heart out of me. How hard it was to write those things down. There are adults now and yet I still ache in remembrance.

Having severe osteo-arthritis and the cartilage in rough shape, I opted to use my medical coverage to get injections of cartilage. Figuring that I might as well do both knees the same day I proceeded. Now who in their right mind reduces travel and commitment of time by doing two knees at once??? The last of the three sessions of injections was the worst. Hearing your doc go "Whoops" is not a good omen. He missed the spot. Thankfully the freezing held. Plus, I also agreed to have coffee with my friend after the first session. The freezing starts to come out of both knees and I'm in agony. I still have a 45 minute drive home. In the middle of Tim Hortons she pulls out her "stash". I'm flustered- "we can't do a drug trade HERE!!! Plus I am an addictions counsellor and you are giving me oxy!!!

I was blessed at this time to have a mental health counsellor with whom I had a hate- love relationship. David would challenge me to do new things as a single parent then be in amazement that I accomplished the task. He wasn't sure he would have done it if he had been in that situation! He had a nice butt- that is why I stuck with him. Ha ha.

In reality I am so apologetic to him and would love to tell him how sorry I am for making his life difficult. I was supersensitive to non-verbal cues and would stop sharing if I saw so much as a whisker move. He went beyond the call of duty, even visiting me at home after the back surgery. He was my mentor and many times I tried to emulate him. He was the best when I loved him: he was the pits when I hated him! He was a bachelor and we often just gabbed about the single life! I am so very sorry for intentionally making your clinical life hell! I was falling in love with you!

It is what it is.

Getting a good mental health counsellor is a challenge. Too many are set on their agendas and really don't take the time to listen. I had one who was hearing impaired and she would assign me homework. The hearing was an issue. At the next appointment she never followed up on assignments and repeated the questions I answered the previous week. Did she not hear or simply didn't listen? Of course as the client YOU are deemed non-compliant. They never close a file saying they are incompetent!!! My advice is to fight, fight and fight until you get the right connection.

Now I am a wimp. I closed off my Mental Health Worker, Stefan in fear I would get attached to him. I enjoyed our banter sessions. I benefitted from resources for sure. But after devastation of David leaving I was taking the pre-emptive stance. Lose Stefan before he leaves me.

It is what it is.

CHAPTER TWENTY-ONE

After the back surgery, I was not so sure I could safely use my body to earn money as a HSW so went back to school in Cornwall. I think I was the oldest student in the class, but there were others close to my age. I was elected class rep and my best friend was the youngest in the class – 17 year old Pierre. My kids were a tremendous help- most times.

I had given each a row in the garden to weed and that night little Daniel says his row was weeds with red balls on the end. Oh dear me!!!! My beets. He pulled every one of them. We ate beets day after day!

Then I asked them one week to pick all the ripe tomatoes. They were to bring the tomatoes into the house so I could can them that night. Heavens forbid- the wheelbarrow was in the kitchen loaded with tomatoes!!!! Don't ask what time I finished canning, but a wheelbarrow in the kitchen!!!! Tomatoes are a different story. Pregnant with my third child, I elected to reduce the salt in the canning process because I had pre-eclampsia in the other two pregnancies. That is a no-no. We all had food poisoning so badly!!

The kidlets kept me hoping. If it wasn't one thing it was another. One thinks you have explained things effectively and then the topic re-surfaces. Each time a child enters a new developmental stage they gain new perspectives on understanding things. That is why we have to repeat that which we thought was sufficiently covered, like divorces. Try that with four kids!

I tried to encourage them to keep up weeding the flowerbeds. They assured me they were. Once I got semi-mobile I noticed a hen and her chicks heading to the flowerbed. Inside the conglomerate of weeds and flowers she had a nest!!! Yep 21 days of incubation and they never knew!!!

Listening can save unwarranted embarrassment. Everyone was hunkered down for the night except the younger two boys laughing and carrying on. I yelled, "Calm down!" Chris had gone to the washroom and yells back. "They are all gone!" I'm confused so ask him to stop in my bedroom on his return to his bedroom. He does. I ask him, "What do you mean they are all gone?" He says the condoms are gone-What???? He explains he used them all. Now why would rational thinking believe I needed a condom when I was in bed alone? I did not want an explanation as to how he used them all. Miscommunication can be embarrassing and yet, oh so revealing!

So many times my neighbors, esp. friend Karen made all things possible. I can't believe the current meme/saying now defames KAREN!!!! She has been the port in the storm on so many occasions. She always did and continues to present clarification, affirmation and just a listening ear without judgement.

Final year of the two year college program was extremely rough on me personally. I had been dating this really nice guy who was reserved but enjoyed gardening etc. I took him to our school Christmas party where unfortunately he drank a lot. He was totally wasted by the time I left to drive us to our respective homes. Apparently he was jealous of me dancing with the younger students!! I rushed into his house, upstairs to the bathroom. I had to pee so badly. As I was leaving the bathroom, doing up my pants when he grabbed me and sodomized me, then passed out. Man oh man I grabbed my boots and ran out of the house to drive home in sock feet and no coat on. Shaking I was going to call the police but thought I was stupid enough to go to the bathroom in his house, it was my fault. That was the end of that. He did call and left a message that he felt like he had run over someone's puppy dog, and could we still get together? Technically not even a sorry to me.

Toute fini!!!!

CHAPTER TWENTY-TWO

That last college year was continually fraught with angst. My 15 yr. old daughter had been sexually assaulted in our house by a chap who was a nurse and ball coach plus attended an Evangelical Church. He thought he would be a good catch for me and financially things would be better. It did not take long for me to feel he was "yet another child "to mother." I became frustrated with his persistence of a relationship. Chris was attracted to his interest and assistance in restoring cars.

Sitting under the apple trees, enjoying the campfire, he and I even spoke of molestation. I told him I'd personally kill anyone who messed with my kids. The bastard waited till I took Chris to work then scooted up to Simone's room before George and Daniel came home from school. She was at home on pain killers after badly bruising her hand under a rock. When I came back 20 min later he was fast asleep on her bed and she was at her desk. I had an uneasy feeling and that night at bedtime told her if he does anything inappropriate tell me. Nothing was said.

The following week he shows up with his two girls and sends all kids but Simone upstairs to the playroom. He demands Simone make him breakfast. I had driven Chris to work. He fondled her while I was away. Sunday she was curled up in a fetal position and hands me a note. I knew something was amiss and as soon as I found out she had been molested, it was off to the hospital with her. Talk about tears, fear, shock, you name it, I felt it. Deep down I felt so proud she was able to tell me,

The nurse and female doc at the local hospital were so gentle and recommended CHEO for the rape examination. Of course Children's Aid is called because she is 15. They come to investigate. They saw I had had the police involved and knew things were under control and no danger was present. Now the interrogation for the victim's statement was gut- wrenching. Listening to Simone graphically describe everything he did to her. My poor child. I cried. I bawled my eyes out but tried to be strong in her presence.

Supposedly he was coming out to work on a car with Chris and when he arrived Chris was to call police. As life happens Chris was on the toilet when he arrived! So making some excuse, he runs across the street to the neighbors to make the call. Police arrive to arrest him and all he says is "shit happens".

I was driving home when the detective was actually in front of me driving slowly- I go to pass and this man waves me over. I stop full of anger. I am told the arrest is happening right now so take a drive allowing at least half an hour before I go home. I want to go home and KILL him myself. Simone begs me not to go home. I don't. That was in June. Later a psychologist says I probably would have drawn blood but would have stopped when blood flowed. I'm not so sure.

Ya-"shit happens!"

Her dad simply said she is not pregnant so what is the big deal. She started school and felt everyone was looking at her. They must know. I try to convince her it is because she is tall, blonde and beautiful. In late Sept she wanted to commit suicide so I had her hospitalized at CHEO. Since I had re-decorated her room, everything was packed in boxes, and only because her desk drawer fell open, did I see the note. That tore me apart. I froze in fear. Sure enough in the old barn she had the rope tied onto a beam. The stool was in position to step off. She was ready to hang herself!

Talk about nightmare on Elm Street!

Parents told me the psychiatrist at the Children Hospital (CHEO) will make you feel like everything is your fault. I'm confident this will not happen to me as sexual assault is the issue. This doc looked like the custodian, nothing professional about her attire or attitude. She in fact had ripped off Simone's hospital identification bracelet when the child refused to talk. A custodian would have had more empathy and diplomacy!

When I followed up 5 days later she had not done any assessments or tests. This was a locked ward. Simone had days of intense frustration and anxiety. I asked if she could connect with the Sexual Assault team from that same hospital. "Nope," not unless I came in and took her down (one floor) to the meetings. Well, being in school with the other kids at home that was not feasible. Although I was able to, almost every day, come in and take her outside for a walk in the late evening. This kid was an outdoors kid: into running and sports, and here she was locked up.

One Friday night the group of youth was watching "The Juror"- a story about sexual assault. Totally inappropriate for a victim of sexual assault to have to watch!! Where was the professionalism? Who provided follow-up counselling after watching that film? Instead they were expected to go to bed!!!!

Then the psychiatrist felt Simone was not getting enough attention and should be in foster care. Well mathematically she was the only girl so yes she got less time than the boys collectively. No-one could identify where I was falling short. We could see her visibly go into a trance repeating the desire to go into foster care, but when we snapped our fingers or some other distraction, she would cry, saying she wanted to be at home. The doctor felt that as a single parent she had problems raising one, so I couldn't do it with four. That is a perfect case of inappropriate transference.

Feeling so judged I questioned my parenting skills, I, in tears called good old Karen for affirmation! This bitch of a doctor annoyed me. She almost destroyed me. This incompetent, arrogant doctor was not providing proper care for my child. Taking the courses about assessments, counselling and rapport, I knew she was slothful.

My counsellor David told me, no-one takes on a psychiatrist. I said "Watch me." I eventually had her removed from staff there. When Simone had meltdowns, they had a male companion to monitor her one to one- even going to the bathroom. You tell me if that sounds appropriate or professional directive? Number one rule in sexual assaults NEVER give the victim a counsellor of the same sex as the perpetrator. I called Children's Aid to report the impropriety. That was soon remedied!!!!

It is what it is.

CHAPTER TWENTY-THREE

Around the fifth month of being in the hospital, Simone's main counsellor asked if she could go on the ski trip with the unit. Now this followed on the heels of her being on lock down and on one-to-one supervision when she had "disappeared".

I was in exams and didn't go in but called to say good night to her when they told me of her escape. Supposedly they had gone next door (Ottawa General) for a "candy" run but wouldn't give any details to me as to how she escaped their watchful eye. Somehow she and another girl slipped away.

I took Colleen whom I was studying with, and my other friend and we booted it to Ottawa always watching for her along the way. Perhaps she was coming home. For some unknown reason, when we got to the ward floor, the idea of Rideau Centre filtered through my mind. The Lord at work!!!!

Off we drove. Unfamiliar with downtown, I could see the Rideau Centre but couldn't find my way in. There was a "Do not enter" sign, and amid the squeals of my passengers not to go in that way, we zipped in!!! To me if a cop caught us, that cop could help locate the girls. We found the two girls but they ran from us. Of course nobody knows if she is genuinely my daughter so the cleaning staff chose not to help. Catching up I knee dropped Simone, getting my friend to sit on her and went off to the other girl who had collapsed.

She had overdosed on Tylenol's but my daughter took less, so was still conscious. Overdoses on Tylenol's can destroy the kidneys.

911 were called.

An ambulance took them to CHEO. Let's add more insult to injury. The emergency staff asked ME what meds she is on. Very sarcastically I said, "Ask 6ᵗʰ floor". Those ass wipes and confidentiality policies: I had run out of patience.

So I'm adamant she cannot go on the ski trip. Gil her counsellor personally takes on the responsibility of informing me in detail, if anything happens. Simone pleads that success on the ski trip is instrumental in her discharge. I relent and off she goes for the day of skiing. I return from school and there is a message to call Gil.

Scared shitless, I call.

Gil comes on to tell me there has been a ski accident on the slope and at that moment, Simone is either in Maniwaki hospital or on her way back to CHEO. Feeling oh so angry, scared and worried, I tell the boys I'm going into Ottawa. Again I'm speeding into CHEO to await her arrival. She arrives by ambulance shortly after I did. Dislocated shoulder, broken wrist, torn leg ligaments and possible concussion. Later Simone tells me "you should have heard the staff. Each was shaking their head, "nope I'm not calling the mother, nope not me".

Apparently it was the last run and the poor gal probably out of shape from being cooped up, crashed into a tree. She said everywhere she looked there was part of her body wrapped around this tree.

It is what it is.

Oh the interest does not stop there. George had been mosh dancing in the living room with some friends. He hurt his big toe. That was Saturday evening. I go ahead to see Simone once the toe is bandaged. Sunday his toe is still oozing, so I take him to the local hospital. He had fractured his toe. The bone had come out and gone back in. They sent us off to CHEO. He is admitted for a week to receive intravenous antibiotics. Nothing like having two kids in the same hospital at the same time, just floors apart.

It is what it is.

CHAPTER TWENTY-FOUR

Now the college exams for me suffered somewhat with all this additional stress. In a response to one of the exam questions I referred to a Briggs & Stratton instead of a Briggs Myers test! Teacher was gracious. Briggs & Stratton was the type of spark plug I needed for the lawn mower. Eventually my daughter returned home and I graduated with Honors. Get that- with honors!!!!

Oh yes, during this time, the ex had called Children's Aid Society (CAS) indicating that I was neglecting the boys by going to Ottawa so much. Not that he visited Simone in the hospital or helped out in any manner, shape or form!! Gr-r-r …. Well they were quite impressed that I got home from school, made a hot dinner, and of which left overs went to school the next day with the boys. I ate my supper on the way to Ottawa.

They had clean clothes, etc. It added embarrassment to the plate when a Social Worker pulled the boys from class to question them. She asked them what they had for lunch. Suspecting crackers and cheese, she was taken back when they said lasagna and garlic bread, a muffin and an apple. They found out I was proficiently fulfilling my parental role.

My sister was visiting and CAS were called again by my ex. He saw a truck so assumed I was jeopardizing Simone's wellbeing by having a man overnight. RAT!!!! Scumbag!!!!!

No he did not help out in any fashion! Nor did the paternal grandparents assist, even though they lived close by. Again it was Karen- my true source of help. Years later I encountered the grandparents at the hospital. Outside the grandpa asked to shake my hand. Suspecting a trick, I was hesitant. He said, "Your kids are my best grandkids. All the thanks go to you. I know you raised them on your own. Well done!!!'

Hell does freeze over!

It is what it is.

CHAPTER TWENTY-FIVE

The trial was hellish. It was hellish for everyone involved and for those watching.

First the glass shield they put up so the victim can't see the perpetrator was backwards. She shook so violently the entire witness stand rattled. I was "kept" in a different room and could hear her sobbing. I could not go to comfort her. My heart broke over and over and over. These shady characters who were in court came to me, offering to do him in but my daughter's Big Sister who also was a cop, advised me not to go that route. I kept their number just in case he got off.

The prosecuting attorney asked Simone what the difference between a nightmare and reality was. She told them a nightmare you wake up from: reality is still there and this was reality. I'm so proud of her!

Then he was testifying how I ran around the house naked. My sister and her hubby were present, they reacted negatively and Karen leaned over telling them remember the source. They went back home and my dad on his death bed asked about it. She was the only person present who could have said anything. I certainly didn't because I was not in the courtroom. I was kept separate from my daughter and anyone else who was testifying. To this day I refuse to trust that sister. I find she is manipulative and others will attest to that. She causes divisions and secures situations to her own benefit. Deep down this control and manipulation simply reflects her insecurity and low self-esteem. It hurts to be victimized again.

The defense attorney had uncovered other victims who testified. One mom died expectantly just before that trail. This man was scary. Although they threw out the testimonies as irrelevant, yet the information of his past was disclosed. Once you hear something, you don't just un-hear it. He got his just dues well, minimally, really in context of what he did. His reign of terror ended when he met us. His conditions upon release from jail means no involvement with anyone under 16, not to be near parks and not to be within 500 metres of Simone or I, our residence or place of work! He'd be a fool to try. Just saying.

"Shit happens!"

It is what it is.

Now I was speechless when my mom called one night of the trial. She just wanted me to be sure nothing of my experiences came out during the trial. After all an older brother was in an influential position and the disclosure wouldn't be "good" for his reputation! He wasn't even the perpetrator! Excuse me- up to this point, she alleges she knew nothing of what happened to me?????

Right to her death bed she negated me. I can't figure this out. I tried my best to help her with whatever I could. I took her out of the senior's home to meals and to shop when no other family member did. Being in a wheel chair was difficult for her to maneuver. The family dynamics remained strained and only selective information was passed on. Again being obscure and secretive does not fly with me! Control to maintain control and power was the operative game.

When she was in rehab building up strength for prosthesis, I did her laundry. Giving up I returned to her room, reporting I can only find one sock. Nonchalantly she says, "That is all I wear these days!" I totally forgot about the amputation of her leg!

I never bought into the negative controlling family dynamics. I called the shots as I see them. At the end we were all gathered around her bed taking turns holding her hand - she pushed mine away. I will never forget that. How hurtful!

Returning to those dysfunctional family dynamics, there was more to add insult to injury; Simone had gone to see her grandpa during a family get-together. He was sexually inappropriate with her. He wanted to show her where to pinch a penis to stop the sperm from coming out.

Again I was deemed the badass. There was no communication. No one told my family that Grandpa, was acting out sexually towards my mother. When some learned Simone had gone up to visit him, they panicked about what may happen, yet still said nothing. I phoned around when we got back home warning all my nieces and nephews to not let the kids be alone with Grandpa because of his actions. One sister took a hissy fit- yes THAT sister. My mom disturbed by what he had done called the police. Simone did not want to press charges. She was sixteen and could make that decision herself. The cops visited and removed my mother from the home for her safety. Never again did they cohabit but were deemed an involuntary separation. No-body talks about that. My family more specifically I, was accredited with the uproar.

After my partner passed, and after my mom passed, I consulted a psychic who could communicate with the deceased. She told me, my mom appreciated me putting the cold cloths on her forehead. How did she know I did that? Plus my mom was saying she was sorry- she should have protected me when I was young! I believe in that psychic's ability. There is no logical way she could have unearthed such information and certainly no way she would have relayed my mom's words unless she truly connected with the spirits.

That psychic blew my socks off. I told absolutely no one I was going. I argued with myself that the money was better spent on groceries. I was so determined to connect with my late partner. He died suddenly from a heart attack. He had gone shopping for my Christmas gift and never made it back home. How shocking to see the police at the door. To this day I don't know how the officer wormed his way inside, but he did. He tells me parts and I'd zone out. I'd repeatedly ask if he was joking. I was in shock. This is Dec 9th. Proof shopping for a woman can kill a guy!!!

The psychic could tell me so much and validated she was indeed communicating with him. She could share things no-one else knew- his favorite sandwich, favorite music, and other health problems. We, meaning the neighbour and I, had taken his garden tractor "Little Red" and made it into a planter in his favorite clump of trees. She shared how please he was with that. There were so many other personal revelations. I knew she had the ability to connect. What an experience!

So many Christians see psychics as evil. I believe if you let it rule your life instead of God, it is erroneous. Just as

Joseph, David and other Bible characters could interpret dreams, humans today can also connect. I truly believe God gives people the ability to do this. She prays for guidance prior to a read.

According to her, my partner really like the poem, "If Tomorrow Should Start Without me" by David Romano, we had for his farewell. She could describe the bouquet of flowers his daughter sent as well as the color of the roses I had sent.

While my dad was in the hospital he requested me to visit. I went. He said he hoped someday I would find my place in the family. He maintained I had no right to stir up trouble as I had done. After all in his mind he was trying to be helpful to Simone. His aging mind could not distinguish what was erroneous behavior. In the psychic readings he was present and did not want to connect.

I've spent my life just trying to find one man to love me as I am. Insanity is when you repeat the same patterns hoping for a different result. I keep going back home looking for love. It is not there. I do not know where it is in human form. I have had jobs that built me up. Working for a farm family, at restaurants, daycares and I social service fields have all empowered me. I may not have shared my troubles but the affirmation built my self-esteem. God is great but sometimes I need those human arms to hold me and that human voice to whisper, re-assuring me I am loved.

I am overwhelmed at the independence of my kids. I miss those days of communication and affection. Life travels on, with each having their own family, careers and community involvement that leaves their old Mom behind. I feel lonely and alone.

Many times I feel overwhelmed and uncertain of the next steps. Yet, I soldier on. I'm the first to say "I love you" to family members. I continue to reach out and it often feels my bio-family is reclusive. Wow-w-w having Irritable Bowel Syndrome (IBS), being alone can be beneficial! There are the usual cramps, bloating and flatulence that plague your daily activities. Just recently I had the runs and knew I had to quickly get home. Pedal to the metal and I reach home in time to dash into the house. I bolt into the bathroom off the foyer. Yes I made it- I'm sitting down letting gravity take over when WHAT- WHO IN HELL IN MY HOUSE LEAVES THE LID DOWN!!!!!

It is what it is.

CHAPTER TWENTY-SIX

Understandably, I would develop mental health issues that manifested in my teen years. At first it was just profound sadness and a lack of hope plus generalized anxiety that felt like fear. Every Monday night I'd come home from school with a massive headache. I was a restless sleeper with reoccurring nightmares. I was a sleep walker and sleep talker. Mental illness has a genetic pre-disposition and it helps to understand what meds worked for others, but in a closed mouth family, it is worse than pulling teeth!

My paternal aunt shot herself when she was in her forties, and that was a taboo subject. Many years later I came to understand her hubby was an abusive alcoholic. In those days without support systems she felt she had no other escape, so she ended her life. I hate secrets. Secrets have negative effects. When asking her daughter about the suicide, I was told blatantly and bluntly, to let it be and not to speak nor inquire about it. Up to her death, the subject was taboo and consequently, our once close relationship disintegrated.

Suffering from mental illness especially depression has not been easy. Trying to explain it to someone who has never experienced it is impossible. When I hear my doc's nurse share her belief that suicide is a selfish act, it irritates me. A woman in her position and with such an attitude prevents folks from getting help. I wrote an article for Canadian Mental Health that many said captures the feelings. The article was published in their newsletter and presented at workshops on depression.

The article follows:

BEFORE THE SUICIDE

Mental illness is an insidious disease and with it comes the probability/possibility of death through suicide. As diabetics' battle diabetic coma and other deficiencies in the body promptly causing body closures/shutdowns, so we must view mental illness as the disease that is possibly worse than cancer, when in its manic state.

Mental illness still has a negative societal image and response. People assume the afflicted has a choice of succumbing to depression. They are not aware that the chemical imbalance limits the choices as you may perceive them.

So many articles talk about the grief families feel after someone has committed suicide and the blame they assume. We don't hear how the victim feels prior to making the choice to end their suffering. Normally it is because no one has picked up on the cues death is imminent. Being someone who suffers from chronic depression, in addition to having an anxiety disorder and other physical problems like diabetes, osteoarthritis, fibromyalgia, obesity, SAD, PTSD and degenerative disc disease for a few, I'm hoping I can shed some light on how "we" feel in those darken hours.

I have felt suicidal and been on the verge of taking the step. I have my plan and things are in order.

At this time the possibility increases as I feel my kids are grown and two of four are not speaking with me because they can't handle my negativity,, my grandkids are estranged, I'm on disability unable to work, I'm living alone, I'm isolated, and I don't want to live a life of continuous pain and sorrow. Rest assured I see a psychiatrist, mental health home support worker, a therapist, a physiotherapist- you name it and I've been diligent in following advice but nothing is alleviating my mental distress. It is bearable most days but some days it slips over the line of adaptability.

When I am really feeling depressed I slip into that mode of "no-one loves me I am worthless" probably as a result of those formative years of being abused and ignored. As Mother Teresa wrote- "Loneliness and the feeling of being unwanted is the most terrible poverty." But recalling the abuse/neglect is manageable often by focusing on my friends and my learned coping techniques to counter the poor choices adults made in not protecting me.

I speak of yet another deeper depressive state. That pit of depression is much deeper than the pit of angst one feels when someone has posed a situational problem that you are torn in determining the "proper" course of action. Those times you feel totally overwhelmed, confused, full of feelings that swirl through and through your head, and the ability to think clearly is impossible.

I am intellectual and totally cognizant of problem solving techniques, and will admit sometimes, perhaps even often, situational problems depress me but not to that terrible pit of darkness that precedes committing suicide. That particular feeling is so painful that when you are not there you (even

I) have difficulty comprehending how bad it is to be there. SO how can anyone else understand the dreadful emptiness and pain-the immense feeling of emptiness and yet so full of hopelessness? You have absolutely no ability to recall the good times. It is like a black hole- slowly suffocating you and pressing your chest to your stomach = tying your heart and head into knots, no way to neither release it nor escape from it.

Suicide is seen as the only option to alleviate the pain for ourselves and is not a reflection of someone not doing enough for us. It is a <u>Chemical Imbalance</u> in the brain that totally overpowers the soul. We need relief and we need resolution- and that option is often death. It is in response to feeling we are a burden to others, to feeling abandoned by life itself and not able to continue on.

Folks have told me to believe in God and I do. Believing in God means I believe Jesus died on the cross for my sins and that He understands my illness and offers me a new life. After all Judas ended his life and had committed to believing in Jesus so suicide is not a foreign scriptural concept. Look at the angst David spoke of in the Psalms. Jesus cried out on the cross- "My God- have you forsaken me?"

Immediately one promotes medication for treatment, and if medication works then that pit is avoided. For me and for others the right combination of meds has not been found. I'm personally tired of being a guinea pig- just trying to hold on. I endure the stigma of chastisement for not working because of my invisible disability.

I endure enough of my own sadness around the fact I can no longer do the things I used to do. I was a very competent professional up to four years ago. I'm great at putting on faces. I can call my friends and to them everything is good but then cry my eyes out after hanging up because I wasn't able to tell them how badly I am feeling... not that they can do anything- I know they care and will be sad but I know they will understand my choice to deal with my pain.

Knowing I have the option of relief through suicide actually helps me cope- I've made a pact with myself not to do anything unless the feeling lingers over 7 days consecutively. Recent side effects of an anti-inflammatory had me hovering at day 5 before I realized it was the side effects of a new medication that was changing the dynamics in my body. Again told to "play' with the medication to verify that was indeed the reaction and it was for me to be cognizant of needing a change in meds...

Luckily or perhaps unfortunately, I am very sensitive to what my body feels and am in tune to these changes medications create. How do I cope? I set deadlines for me- let's make it to the end of whatever month it is and if nothing changes I will say goodbye to life or the hell hole I live in.

I had to switch family doctors because my GP insisted I can get through this and to persevere not realizing and accepting how ill I was. That was a tough time as I had a close relationship (29 yrs) with that doc but fortunately the new one seems cognizant of my inability to just "snap out of it". Again left without true support and now my psychiatrist has left his practice and I fall through the cracks with no referrals. My one friend asks "how crazy are you?" when she discovered I was a Royal Ottawa patient – "you seem normal

most times"... how do I explain the illness with such an inferred sense of "craziness" associated with being mentally ill? The stigma and fear of "I'm going to kill someone" if I am mentally ill makes me keep silent about my pain and illness. Most mental illnesses do not result in murder! People need to realize there is a wide variance of the illness in types and severity.

What else would help? Being nonjudgmental and just sitting and listening to me talk would be a start- let me talk about suicide and how I think it is the answer- don't tell me not to do something stupid because I'll agree not to do something stupid. You need to be cognizant suicide is not feeling like a stupid option at that time.

Tell me and show me that you are supportive of me, love me and promise you will be there no matter how ugly it gets. Do you know how many friends abandon you when you are depressed? It is taxing to filter through the negativity and reactivity being expressed.

In all the years of my depression and especially the past 4 only 1 cousin actually asks how I am and really means it! Family avoids talking as if it is contagious and that just isolates me further. But in reality my family has never been super close to me anyways due to labelling me as a "mental case" and a "wayward child" - it has been over 10 years since a sibling visited me in my home.

I need you, family and friends to call me- visit me, show that I am valuable even though I am sick, and forgive me for wrongs you think I may have committed. Come sit with me as we do nothing.

Question if doctor assisted death is that any different than me committing suicide? Be mindful of what you say in public places – like- "suicide is selfish" get yourself some training in the mental health field before you shut anyone else down. Please understand my distress!
-end of article.

One of my greatest regrets was not keeping a record of the medications I was on. The psychiatrist would often give me samples so there were no pharmacy records. It would have been best if I had a small notebook and wrote down each med and the side effects. No meds work the same for each person. Down through the years with different doctors: I can't recall the names and effects. There is no continuum of records and no-one suggested to me to keep records.

It is what it is.

I continue to struggle with additional health problems. The diabetes has been maintaining acceptable readings since Ozepic was added. Injecting once a week isn't too bad. Because of the temporary side effects of dizziness, headaches and nausea, I simply count on that day being a "nothing" day. However, Saturday the sugars plummeted me to a 3. Whew- what a reaction! Intense sweating, dizziness, severe headache, blurred vision and just not doing well. My thirteen year old granddaughter successfully contacted telehealth who sent an ambulance to fetch me to the hospital. The reasons for the sudden plunge are unknown but perhaps because of a twenty pound weight loss the medications had to be reduced. Trial and error!

Now I need to find a vial to carry some maple syrup with me. Liquids enter your blood stream faster. Also the "rocket" candies are recommended. Can I keep out of them? Hallowe'en is the time to buy!

It is what it is.

CHAPTER TWENTY-SEVEN

Today being 2020, there still remains a stigma around mental illness. Treatments are hit or miss. The wait times to get services are notorious. When you call, you are in distress weeks ago and finally get nerve enough to call now. Who wants a six month waiting period for help? Then the gauge is whether you are "bad" enough for a particular service. Psychiatrists are questionable themselves. I had one who had his office darkened completely except for a small desk lamp. The bugger fell asleep every time shortly after I arrived. I'd walk out. Two days later the secretary would call to book another appointment. Am I that unimportant?

Another one, similar atmosphere, but would always say "what does your husband do? "I'd say I have been divorced for 6 years- there is no husband." "Excuse me- read the damn file- I am divorced with no help from the father". Can't YOU remember!

Yet another would ask me the same questions so I would go in and automatically answer the questions, get up and leave, I booked an appointment for next week. I quit and asked the family doc for another referral. I was told I was non-compliant and couldn't keep changing psychiatrists.

It is what it is,

It takes so-o-o long to come off a med and start a new one. It takes time to find the right one or combination for oneself. I had a med that made me sleep all the time; others resulted in REALLY strange dreams. For instance I recall dreaming I was disfiguring toddlers, cooking them in the oven and then trying to put them back together again. This was SO unsettling and emotionally disturbing for me. It nearly made me puke.

Now since I fell through the cracks of the system when my psychiatrist left the hospital, my care landed on my family doctor. Apparently I was not sick enough to warrant a transfer of file but still in need of monitoring. So my doc puts me on lithium, one of the older drugs. First I am disoriented during the night. I can't find the bathroom until my son directs me to the right room. Shortly afterwards on another night, I find my way, feel the porcelain on the back of my knees, and I plunk myself down. Crash- boom-ouch. I had landed in the Jacuzzi tub. I was stuck in a V formation. With my son's help I get routed around and out. I cause tissue damage to my upper spine and mid back. The doc is sure this will balance itself out. I am still weepy so he ups the Lithium to three tablets at bedtime. I'm struggling at nighttime with dreams that I am acting out, continuing to end up on the floor. Still I cannot get up because of the knee replacement. This particular night I dream I am at my friend's and have to go to the washroom. She tells me her hubby is in the shower so I have to use her downstairs washroom. I never have been to her downstairs but off I go. Yes I did peek into the upstairs washroom, and yes hubby was in the shower. Great view! So downstairs I go to find what I called a hobbit bathroom with multiple sections to the door and varying locks. I eventually crawl in and relieve myself. Getting back out was a problem. I was shouting for help. Yes, my son came to my aid. I was on the floor with carpet burns from crawling into and out of this perceived tiny washroom. I had soiled myself. Again the neighbor has been called for help in getting me up. It was all a hallucination that I was acting out.

Into the shower I go, and yet know how to dress myself and do basic hygiene. Now if my son had not videotaped me I would have zero knowledge of what transpired for the remainder of the night. I was in the kitchen having tea and toast while I waited for the ride to the airport. I was seeing people in the living room, calling them by name. Two others were coming through the ceiling and no I did not want them there. I'd be waving my hand at them to go way. I could spell their last name and knew where they resided. Seemingly I didn't know my son other than he was a reporter. He was the one who selected the radio/TV the stations on CKBY-CJET-CJOH, that were viable back in the day!.

I believed I was going over to Lizzie's granddaughter's wedding reception. Kate and William would pick me up at the airport. I didn't need a dress because the Queen was going to give me one of hers. Chris talked me into a rest before the excitement on the plane. I treated our spare bedroom like a hotel room. I checked out all the drawers! I settle in bed and in a flash I am dressed in a dress that I couldn't have told you its location, with the matching bolero and the tights. How did that happen and so quickly? Back into housecoat finally and settled in bed for a rest. I sleep. I am aware someone is in the room and ask-"Who is there?" It is my friend Samure who does train dogs. Immediately I wanted to get out of bed to go train Tish's new puppy. She talks me into resting till later. This went on until at least, to six that night.

The first two times I saw the video I laughed till I cried. The third time I sobbed in fear this was my new life. Next visit I made the doctor swear he would administer MAID if I became like that. MAID is "Medically Assisted Intravenous Death. I hated the prospect of life like that. Now I have reduced the Lithium to two pills, one in morning and one at night. It keeps me balanced.

People question how I can be depressed when I am jovial and smiling. Good meds and a sense of humor. You know what **fine** stands for?

F-feed up

I-irrational,

N- Neurotic,

E- emotional,

So how **fine** are you?

Family members don't want to discuss mental health so basically hide from the truths of the illness. I had family member say such and such a cousin has a good hubby, nice home, etc. so why is she depressed? Depression is a chemical imbalance. Sometimes my own family physician falters trying to seek a circumstantial reason for my dips in coping abilities. It is frustrating when he says "your nerves" as opposed to "mental state."

A geriatric doctor insisted I reduce my zopiclone from 2 to 1 at bedtime. I told her one of my triggers is fatigue. If I don't sleep, I get severely depressed then suicidal. Oh, but she was the expert, and I had to follow her recommendations. That was a Tuesday, by Friday my son was begging me to take the other pill and my 11 year old grandson was "Grandma—what is wrong? You are not yourself?" I was trying to hold out till she called but when I receive word a good friend had passed from pancreatic cancer; I simply decided to screw her. I went back onto the two pills. Come to find out from a report she sent to my family doctor, she wanted me off all meds. There was no acknowledgement of my medical situations. I am a diabetic. I have good cholesterol because of the medication I am on.

It is what it is.

Psychiatrically I know what my triggers are and am very aware of my body. I fired her- the insolent twerp! We must remember doctors are working for us. My family doctor and I discussed the reality he was the one who would pick up the pieces if I crashed. I truly felt she had zero respect for my input so it was time to end connections with her! You can't trust medical professionals blindly. Know your body and fight for YOU!!!

My own Mom said if I was right with God I shouldn't be depressed. Let me assure you that according to John 3:16 which states that by accepting Jesus as my savior I am right with God. The devil, Satan causes turmoil and pain and God will use it to keep us close to Him. Bible characters like David suffered from depression-read the Psalms.

I have felt the presence of God very strongly. After I was separated my youngest was ring-bearer in his aunt's wedding. I felt so alone. On the floor of the boys' room I sobbed. Please God show me you care. I felt arms around me.

Then more recently I re-connected with a chap I liked but there always seemed to be negative interference from someone like his ex-wife or his sister. I was going slow redeveloping a friendship, not a relationship, when he texted some weird comments about my mental health. I prayed about the validity of this connection, and all vibes disappeared. I was done with him without regrets. Thank God.

This reminds me of a relatively new friend I made. He was quite handsome, polite and seemed to have a strong Christian faith, so I was interested in learning more about him. When his church closed, he stopped going to church. I've invited him a number of times. Others have too. Was he just dedicated to his birth church?? Well, I did learn he was a talker. I mean talk for 5-6 hours at a time. This is fine in the middle of the day until my phone dies. His conversation is of history of the area so my answers are minimal prompts-ya, oh, uh—hums and so on. Well this particular evening he calls after I've taken my night meds. Four hours into the conversation I hear him shout my name!! Oh my. He asks "Did you fall asleep on me?" I guess I did so he decides to let me go. Now when he calls he always says I better let you go before you fall asleep. I'm sorry.

It is what it is.

With my social anxiety, people don't see the shaking knees, the diarrhea, the tense stomach; they just see the positive presentations. I can put on a good mask. Many times I deflect with humor. It is exhausting keeping up a front. Unless you know me well, the fear/anxiety is not detected.

I was best man in this person's wedding up the valley. I knew five people in total. I was a bundle of nerves. I had asked the minister what happens if she or I drop the rings. Apparently it was my task to run after them but she quickly assures me, it never happens. Lo and behold his ring rolls off her Bible, down the aisle, coming to rest by the register.

Attending guests pass the runaway ring forward to the groom. Whew!

Then before the reception the bride has her nephew drive the groom, matron of honor, and herself into the village for a drink. She purposefully left me behind, in the parking lot alone!!! I was indignant and furious. I wished I had the courage to up and leave. I still drove them to the hotel where I was staying and they had been upgraded to the top of the line room compliments of my son in the hospitality field. That ended that connection. I had been friends probably ten years with him. Yes I had been his girlfriend for 5 years, but pot and alcohol destroyed the connection. Did I need to know the marriage was not consummated that night because he was drunk and high!!!! He claimed he understood my mental illness but she was jealous and set me up. There is nothing I detest more than being alone in a strange place even if it is outside!

It is what it is.

CHAPTER TWENTY-EIGHT

We grew up doing radio Sunday school lessons then went to church when my oldest bro got married. The only thing that interested me was the children's story and the cute guy that sat behind us. Having a major crush on this other guy –the 4-H guy, I went to a non-denominational church where he was speaking. The concept of salvation was new to me. Realizing salvation is like accepting a chocolate bar- it is not mine till I actually take it, I finally accepted Christ as my savior at age 18. I attended faithfully, bringing youth to children's programs for several years.

One Friday night I returned these two sisters to their home, and was invited to the back forty to share in a bonfire with other youth, back in the house I partook of a hot chocolate before leaving. Vaginally I was very sore the next day and I couldn't remember driving home. As gossip runs, it was rumored this chap had "got me" the church go-er by drugging my drink. Now what infuriates me is that to this day, the perpetrator's brother can share another version and his is deemed the "right" story. Even my son sees me as wrong. Who was there- me or them?

It is what it is.

Later I learned hot chocolate is the easiest drink to doctor with drugs. I was running a daycare centre in Ottawa, top position, top paycheck when I realized I was pregnant. I was granted an abortion (back then 1978, it was only by authorization, for you to get one) but I couldn't do that while caring for infants- spiritually nor professionally. Talk about copious prayer. It went against my grain. I turned down the opportunity for an abortion. Co-incidentally no-one had suggested prior to this, that I should even be on birth control.

I was excommunicated from the church and no-one, except one lady supported me. She remains my spiritual mom to this day. She always is encouraging, supportive and a strong Christian. I was scared, lonely, and depressed beyond comprehension. Again the subtle message I was unlovable and unacceptable.

40 some years later several of the congregants still refuse to shake my hand when meeting in public! Some definitely act holier than thou. The head leader's mother confronted me in a grocery store saying, "If I got an abortion, all would be good. The community wouldn't know". Excuse me we are not dealing with image but a real child! The gospel says we will know Christians by their love, and by their actions (fruit). As much as I believe in salvation, that group is more like a cult. Sins are equal in God's eyes. Yet actions/careers of others were subtly questionable and flew under the radar of judgement. How do you lead someone to Christ when you are so cold and unforgiving?

I have never joined a church since. Although at the existing church I inquired twice to join, now I will not EVER subject myself to humiliation of even asking again. True enough, external factors came into play on their part but I stress in my head and heart it is because I am not wanted and unworthy. That creates such an internal loneliness.

I've been hurt by organized religion more than once, yet I believe and trust in God. Another church had me very involved as Sunday school superintendent/teacher, Vacational Bible School Co-coordinator, and then when I separated from my abusive husband, they vanished. Neighbors with no religious affiliation helped me the most. That made me very sad.

The minister from there surfaced many years later in the church I was attending and acted as if he hardly knew me. I was very involved in that church as well, had surgery and not a soul even touched based with me during five months of being absent. That minister, perhaps as a joke said my singing stopped his beard from growing. That hurt. Then he divulged something in a church service, using my name, disclosing something I had said in confidence. I left there. I just hate being hurt. Fortunately I now have a warm inviting church. I still keep my walls up.

The walls of sensitivity continue to limit me in what I share. For this reason I write under a pen name and maintain being anonymous. My dreaded fear is family will still negate what happened to me. I physically burned with embarrassment and unrest just giving the manuscript to two people to read to deem whether it is worth proceeding or if it is only for my own eyes. I project confidence but lack confidence!

Now if you want to hear of co-incidence, in this "new" church I wanted to be friends on Facebook, with the lady who sat behind me. Problem was her origin was listed as where I also went to school. Her husband tells me he had so-and-so as a 4-H leader: did I know him. I replied- "I can better you on that one- I had him as a 4-H leader and as a brother!!" We enjoyed reminiscing of folks but I had to keep reminding him of the age difference. Small world after all.

It is what it is.

CHAPTER TWENTY-NINE

Going back to the pregnancy, I vowed I would give the child up if it was a boy. I was sure a male child would remind me of the father and that would be too hard on me. Once I met my son, wee Chris, he melted my heart. He and I bonded. I loved him immediately.

It was so funny when he was circumcised. He slept through feeding time, so nurses felt next one to cry would be him and they would bring Chris in to me. So it happened, the wee tyke was crying so hard I immediately latched him to my breast BUT his face seemed too red, his hair too spikey. I unwrapped the blanket just in time to hear the nurses whispering- "Oh no we gave her the wrong baby." By this time I am reading the bracelet- this is not my child. Humiliation reigned on all of us. How could I not know right off it was not my child? And how could the nurses give me the wrong baby!!!!

Believe it or not when pictures were done at say three months of age the photographer mixed up the pictures of the two boys. I think I have the right child but sometimes I wonder!!

I went on to meet my husband- what a mistake that was. He was a first generation immigrant and by European descendant tied to parent's apron strings. With a two hr. long distance relationship I was unsure of things- I always had headaches on Sunday nights after being on his farm, which I attributed to stress. Come to find out after marriage I was very allergic to feathers. THAT was disastrous, living on a poultry farm.

I went for my allergy shot for the first time since getting married. I had such a negative reaction the doctor questioned if this was me, right serum, etc. After all we were new to each other. I was shivering and shaking so much he put his winter jacket over me. I worsened! LOL his jacket was down-filled and so began a history of events over the next 29 years with that doc.

My allergy specialist- Frankish was more than kind and accommodating esp. when I was taking bee serum to build up my resistance to bee stings. Seven wasp stings netted me hospitalization for ten days. My dearly loved neighbour had taken me to the hospital and wee Daniel aged two hated her for taking me away. Now at 6 feet tall he offers to sit on her knee.

During that time in the hospital, I took my intra-venous with me into the washroom, returned to bed, only to have this old chap across the room climb into bed with me. Frantically I rang for the nurse to get assistance. Next morning I was so nauseated that doc teased me I was pregnant already! Come to find out I had blood poisoning.

Being so out of it, I slept a lot. The doc came during his rounds to wake me up, and groggily, I asked if he had been painting. There was a glob of white in his hair! Later took the boys to Tupper for haircuts and the barber was telling me that exact story that I had just lived. Doc figured he better get his hair trimmed. Take note that I was still married at this time, and it was I, who took the boys to the barber. Uncomfortable being the only female present!!!!

It is what it is!

CHAPTER THIRTY

Now when I think of my choice of Petrus for a husband, I have to realize the key words in life are Choose, Choice and Chose. Those words provide the ownership of every action, thought and word. There is so much power and credibility in using those words. I did not choose wise, so my choice was not good, leaving me wishing I had chosen differently.

Petrus seldom spoke in front of his parents but said things would be different when we were married. Where have we heard that line before? I vividly recall when he arrived once with this long narrow box and I was ecstatic- long stem roses. He came in and proceeded to show me the gun he had just bought! G-r-r ... I should have known.

When given the ultimatum of his buying a farm or getting married, I felt getting out of the single parent stigma was a positive step. I should have, could have and would have walked then but.....choose, chose choice.

It is what it is.

The night before our marriage I stated to friends over cinnamon toast that I was making a mistake but they convinced me I was just experiencing wedding jitters. He had accompanied his family back to their RV site and left me alone with the bridal party from my side of the family. With all the costs and preparations could I have "escaped" from the commitment? Relatives were attending from afar. Oh dear, hindsight is 20/20!

The relationship was emotionally and physically abusive. He never left his parents to cleave to his wife. He would attend his family events while I stayed home with sick kids. When Simone was a flower girl in her cousin's wedding, he didn't even go! She was so cute. His parents would not send gifts to the kids until they came to get them when they were well. Merry Christmas to you, too. I always got tools as a gift from them!!!

Petrus had a habit of letting himself go. He didn't shower, shave or keep himself well-groomed! This was a constant flashback to my sexual perpetrator. This was tremendously hard to manage.

The minister almost didn't baptize our youngest because it was just me bringing the kids to the Protestant church. His involvement was minimal to non-existent. He did start going to church at first but stopped when his brother laughed at him for going. Although his mom sang in the Catholic choir the family had little respect for God, or church, or morals of any kind. It was easy to "hide" behind farm work. Did I mention my brother who attended church was also a farmer? Choose, chose, choice.

Petrus' attention to his family was non-existent. Poor Simone broke her wrist and he never came to mind the kids for me to take her to the hospital... Several weeks later the poor munchkin reacted to bee stings and again the neighbor lady accompanied us to the hospital. She was so sick. She had gone unconscious and vomiting violently with no signs of Petrus even though he was present to witness her reactions. How can someone be so callous???

His doctor told me he had an emotional block. If he committed suicide I was not to take on the responsibility. It was beyond my doing. Alcohol became his solution. His family was well-to-do but we lived on bread crumbs. He always accused me of squandering the money. The kids lived on hand-me down clothes. I was as frugal as possible. One thousand dollars a month for us to live on- a family of six. His momma liked to instruct me on what day to do what and was aghast when I forbid the kids to pick eggs before school. They practiced child labor.

Petrus' nephew was kept home to drive the bulldozer in the fields when he was four- yes an accident waiting to happen. His school would call me about his absenteeism and no lunches so I simply said wrong number and gave the parents/grandparents number.

One day I was driving the bulldozer in the field when the two brothers squabbled about which direction I was to drive. They were plenty ticked when I just turned the machine off, sat there until they concurred which direction I was to go. Last time they did that to me!!! I could and did dig in my heels when pressured.

A later incident, where his bro used the animal probe on his four year old son resulting in the child not walking, Children's Aid Society was involved. The family bought their way out. I was deemed the squealer. I told Petrus because I knew of it I had to speak up when interviewed, or I could lose my professional qualifications as an ECE. His dad and bro came to "visit" and said I would believe it is wrong to put a child's hand on a burner- duh YES.

My psychologist told me as long as I was with Petrus I was "safe: The family would deem it Petrus's responsibility to beat me into submission. No way would I tolerate this behavior and told Petrus if he ever laid a hand on me, the cops would be called. Sometimes I can and do stand up for myself. I always go to battle for my kids.

Mind you this is the same psychologist who told me even if Petrus was a sphinx I was better off to stick with him because I was "unmarketable." I was obese, and with four kids, so no-one would want me. Where did I hear that message before?

Petrus physically choked me the first Christmas after marriage when I was 2 months pregnant, and cracked the door another time when he tried to hit me. I vividly remember his hands on my neck as colored stars floated before my eyes. He physically was a very strong man. He was also an alcoholic and he never was involved as "us". When he said "we" it was his bro and him. In attempts to save the marriage we moved farms and overnight his bro was dictating what building was to be torn down etc. I couldn't even entice him to go out for a coffee to celebrate our anniversary or to celebrate buying the farm. After all I had come up with the winning bid. There were times he hung out with a known homosexual so much I wondered if his preference was guys? Drinking was his favorite activity. Smoking and drinking ate much of the monthly budget.

It is what it is.

As the saying goes: the last nail in the coffin, was when he chose to go on holidays overseas with his parents, leaving us a family of 5, behind. He rarely went on holidays with us. I told him if he went, the house siding color was mine to decide: so yellow siding was up when he returned. His mother and brother wanted white.

He did go with us to the Toronto Zoo one year when school was out, and one summer camping when Simone was a baby. He was a different person when away from his family. Other than that I took the kids camping in Gracefield, Santa's Village in Lake Placid, Brampton and other day trips. The beach was popular with the kids.

I was always told there would be money and time when we were ready to retire. That did not entice me. Now was the time to live with the children being happy and having experiences as children. Sure enough, when the adult brothers sold the farm in their late 50's they both became millionaires. Do you think any of the children got a bit of cash? Of course not. His then wife had a hay-day spending Petrus' portions. Now she is out of the picture.

Twenty-two years after the divorce, I still have vivid nightmares and night sweats of that married life and dysfunctional relationship with the entire family.

People question nature verses nurture. I question whether my kids are the way they are because of genetics. Often I shake my head at their antics. The exclusion and isolation seems nature because I did not raise them to be so selfish and self-centered. One hasn't spoken to me for two years plus. We were so close.

I made so many sacrifices for them. I gave and gave and gave. Now another son seldom connects. If I see him and his family once a year I am fortunate. They live close by. They can't even make a phone call. My other son likes to dominate and control me. It is elder abuse. I put up with it because I can't afford to be independent. He decides what and what not, I can eat. Heaven forbid if I make a decision without consulting him and I must accept his decision. All this compounds my mental well-being. I am at loss how to manage the abuse. Luckily he respects the privacy of my bedroom. He does not physically assault me. Psychologically, verbally and emotionally, he abuses me. Why me??

It is what it is.

CHAPTER THIRTY-ONE

When we first moved into that pig farm place, the neighbor came over to welcome us. My kids always had friends over, so with all eight kids scurrying this way and that, she asked, "Are they all yours?" Those folks were the kindest, most sincere folks one could ever meet. He had been a war pilot, until he crashed his plane near Manotick. As a result, one shoe was built up so he could walk. Uneven ground was a challenge. The two younger boys fought over which one was going to get the newspaper for him before the bus arrived. A system of taking turns alleviated that issue.

George lost his glasses in the snow tunnel just opposite their front window but on my property. We raked, we scoured the area, so Al calls over-"What are you looking for?" I tell him "Spring"!!! We did find the glasses in the spring but poor George is blind without glasses so another pair had to be purchased.

Now I have never had that many pigs in one place, so when the specialist advised soft gentle music to soothe them, I was doubtful. Being me, I put on rock and roll and the pigs went nuts. I frantically ran up and down the aisles sh-h-h-ing them. Never did I repeat that! Living on the farm was good for the kids.

On this farm were two rows of hedges that needed trimming badly. So I bought a hedge trimmer. That Thanksgiving Daniel, probably age four, was aghast at his aunt using hedge trimmers to cut the turkey and scissors in her salad. Nothing like an electric knife and silver plated tong set to get a young man's head going.

That was the same hedge George was stuck in after a tremendous snowstorm that hit out area. Roads were closed to traffic and many events were cancelled. With snow so high the kids went out playing and poor George plopped down into the centre of the hedge. We tried ropes, ladders and combinations thereof before I got him out. Seriously I was at the point of calling 911 for help!!!

One night in mid-February, the kids are in bed when the neighbor calls that my house is on fire. PANIC- but I've just been through the house and there is not a fire. She insists it is the back of my house. In no time I see the flames in the field. I know my kids are in bed but she can't find her young lad. Come to find out the boys had been building a fort in February in this hollowed out old tree during the afternoon. Being cold her lad decided to build a fire. He knew what had transpired so was hiding out in a closet to avoid discipline! The boys were sure it was out but obviously a spark landed and ignited a fire later. The senior neighbor comes over across the field and says, "So we are having a wieny roast, eh?" The sight of a tree burning upright is something else.

Now this neighbor kid liked to hang out at our place. One night I went to bed early not feeling well. Man it was so-o-o cold in the house the next morning when I awoke. I figured the furnace was out. One of the kids went down stairs and in no time was shouting for me. That sweet neighbor boy had not closed the door tightly hence letting snow blow into the house. Every plant I owned was frozen. I think even the artificial ones were stiff. A cactus I had for twenty-five years and six feet high was as limp as…as…as…..

I cried. I sobbed and sobbed.

When we were renovating the place, we found a letter in the walls behind what perhaps, was the medicine cabinet. A daughter was writing home to her mother. She shared "how Auntie had come to visit. It was good to see her arrive but even better to see her leave."

"They left a plate of food on the front step for the Indian that lived in the bush. There were reports of how the family had the summer complaint." If the walls could talk, I'm sure there would have been lots of stories.

Mind you in February, I was stripping the white paint off the door frame into the living room when the odor of skunk permeated the house. According to the neighbor, a skunk had gotten into the house years before, sprayed and the owner simply painted with an oil base paint to smother the smell.

As much as the kids had bronchial problems on the chicken farm, Simone continued with health challenges for a few years. The doctor's receptionist was a bit of a prick. She complained I was calling too often. I had to remind her I was calling on behalf of five people! Speaking with the doctor, I was assured my concerns were valid. I just need the prescription pad!!!

Alas poor wee Simone had her appendix out in grade 2, then in grade 3 had pneumonia in both lungs. The appendix issue was just before Christmas and when Santa said he couldn't set her on his knees because of her surgery, it confirmed Santa was REAL

Santa was a genius. Because the kids were super excited Christmas morning, breakfast was a battle. Then Santa got wise and provided breakfast in the stocking. There was a juice box, and two boxes of those individual cereals plus a fruit. !!!! Gifts under the tree from me could be open after the turkey was in the oven.

Chris decided to test if Santa was real. He tied his bedroom door shut with a two inch gap and put flour on his wood floor. If I was the Santa then I couldn't get in, plus I'd leave footprints. Santa was REAL.

Speaking of Christmas we always made a gingerbread house open for eating on New Year's Day. When they returned from trick or treating on Halloween they sorted through the candy for everything suitable for the gingerbread house decorating- tootsie rolls for chimneys, red and green suckers, chocolate squares, orange corn for the fireplace effect, and licorice for the roof. This reduced consumption, and remained in the freezer until the construction began.

Some say girls are easier to handle. I beg to differ: my girl was the only one to climb the TV antenna to the roof when she was two! She was always climbing and into things.

She also climbed on the kitchen table and ate the centre out of three pumpkin pies while I bathed the two younger boys. Her dad watched TV not bothering to help supervise. She still likes pumpkin pie today!

She was allergic to all major antibiotics so I was worried sick when she had pneumonia. The doc didn't want to admit her to hospital because of exposure to other germs plus she would be upset that things were not familiar as in no mom and no brothers. What a battle to get fluids into her. Eventually we used a blender as the measuring tool. She drank from an eggcup and that equal amount was put in the blender. The goal was to fill the blender. She did not want ice cream, popsicles, or juices and just water was a battle. She made it through. My in-law's never offered to help by getting groceries or treats for her but they did manage to call the Children's Aid Society to report me for not seeking medical care and hospitalization for her! The doctor straightened things out!!!

My third child was a large baby for which the delivery involved an episiotomy. There was lots of tearing and stitches. First morning home, Petrus said you want sex in the morning, there you got it.

Yep I moved out of the bedroom that day. The pain was beyond belief. That was **rape**.

How did the 4th child happen?? A single night of having to sleep in his bed to accommodate overnight guests, and poof, it happened. I went to bed early and after his drinking minimal sex occurred but enough to result in pregnancy. I was so sure I just had the flu. I refused prenatal care until I was five months pregnant. After all how could I be pregnant! Petrus went as far as claiming the child was not his, but the doctor's!!! All three boys have the same winter birth month.

It was hard on Simone when she was young to understand that she didn't get presents because it was not her turn yet. She had to wait till summer like me.

It is what it is.

CHAPTER THIRTY-TWO

Overall life was difficult and tumultuous for my kids, yet full of opportunities. I tried my best despite limitations and financial restraints. Being a single parent was no different than being in a two-parent family where one parent is emotionally and/or physically absent.

I recall poor Chris was wrapped up in the dog's chain and Petrus simply came in for coffee saying the kid was wrapped in the chain. I went out to rescue the poor child. Who in their right mind walks by doing nothing? He could have been killed, or was that the intention?

I'll never forget the sight when nursing the youngest Daniel in the morning; the other three were sitting at the table waiting for breakfast. Petrus simply ate his own never giving the kids as much as a piece of toast!!! If I went to the Ladies Aid meetings of the church the kids would be asleep on the floor in their clothes when I came home with Petrus tucked neatly in bed himself. I hated to go out but I needed socialization.

I was at one meeting when one lady asked where I was from. I told her and she went on to say how her son (deceased) was good friends with a chap that married a lady from there. I acknowledged that was my sister. She covered her mouth with a gasp, asking oh dear what did I say. There was nothing bad. LOL

It is what it is.

I tried to give my kids as many opportunities as I could on such a limited budget. The kids were involved in community events like scouting, guiding, church, Vacational Bible School, holidays like camping with me and sports teams. I kept them as active as possible. In exchange I helped out where I could by giving of my time.

It was Apple Day for the Scouting division. The Legion donated the apples for the lads to sell for funds in return for selling poppies. It was easy to raise nearly one thousand dollars. It was my job to pair off parents and a Beaver, Cub and Scout to do a particular area of town. True enough; the one Scout leader said his brother might stop by to see about borrowing some tool. I did not give it a second thought, just kept going with my job. At the end, this man is left standing so I send him out with a crew. He obliged. When we gathered back at noon, I found out he was the brother and had no intention of selling apples!!! Whoops.

We were on our own for 2 years before the community started to recognize I was a single mom. Everyone was so used to it being me and the kidlets.

All four kids were blessed to have Big Brothers/Sisters match them to wonderful *"Bigs."* Sincere thanks to Chris, Tara, Peter and Don. They encouraged the kids so much. Their father was not involved in their lives so this was additional support for them. Terrific!!!

Other business men in the community advised me the separation would be devastatingly hard for me as the family was known to be ruthless, and unforgiving. Every other marriage had dissolved with this family getting custody of the kids. They believed whoever had the most money could afford the kids and therefore have custody.

I was not only divorcing Petrus but the entire family. Everything was mish-mashed with personal and business as this was a family business. I kept records so when Petrus' father tried to ding me for van payments I had the proof of full payment. Ruthless was a gentle word for the problems they presented.

Petrus and I had agreed to a trial separation and in no time it was a divorce at his father's directive. There was total disregard for us as a family. I was so thankful for support from my friends. At the mediation, Petrus became angry and threatening me. His own lawyer called him a Neanderthal and ordered him to sit down. He wanted to hit me.

Given his finances the settlement was meager but the fight wasn't worth it. This put an end to the threatening phone calls and actions. Many times I was scared, especially if I was alone. I sensed he would not hurt the kids. I knew them to burn down a house and declare innocence, so anything was possible.

I was blessed with professional training in child development and care, so I was up for the battle. I knew I was a good mom, most times, or when in doubt, I called Karen, Trinkie or Tom for affirmation. I often wavered. My bio family never asked once how I was managing. As much as Petrus had adopted Chris I wonder if he would have battled equally for him? Praise God for great friends and my faith.

If Petrus went without speaking to me for 2 weeks it was a good relationship in his books. I was forewarned by my doc such stress would kill me. I prayed that if I had to walk through this door of separation then open the door widely.

After a particularly calm weekend, I was stirring the gravy while making supper, when he announced he would be moving out on Saturday. Yes Lord!! Again, answered prayers. Many times he had said I could leave but not with the four children nor with anything. That was a no go as the kids were my life. I helped him pack; giving the best of everything we had duplicates of. Then after we separated, his mom went through the house claiming items for him. Whatever- just take it.

I will never forgive them for "taking" the kids one day when I was at work. I came home to no dog and no kids. Worried they were in the manure pit; I searched frantically but did find the dog locked in the barn. My neighbors helping to search, recalled a transport leaving the driveway. I went down to the family farm and there they were- visibly upset. George said "I told dad we needed to leave a note, but dad said we'd call when we got to Oma's". Oma would not allow them to use the phone. Poor darlings trusted their dad and were tricked into a false sense of security. That was the one and only time they did that. When trust is broken, it is nearly impossible to regain, even if it is a parent!

They also knew Barkley wasn't to be locked in the barn.

He claims I turned the kids against him but he fails to examine his actions. How many Friday nights did the two youngest wait at the mailbox, with backpacks to be picked up. They cried at dark when I told them to come in to go to bed. Who did the comforting?

Interestingly he got involved with a woman shortly after the divorce, believing two parents were better than one. His lawyer told him to look at what he was bringing in to the fold. She had 4 kids: the oldest in jail in Montreal, 2nd oldest female- pregnant on the streets. 3rd in Burritt's Rapids Correctional Centre and the youngest in CAS care because she threw a butcher knife at him!!!!!! SHE is telling ME how to parent!!!!!!

My kids were so impressed that one of her kids was in a private school where he didn't even have to pour his own cereal. They surmised she must be so rich. Fortunately I stopped in at home at lunch one day, and my oldest said the teacher had called to confirm it was okay for Jay to come home for the weekend. WHAT???

I called the number twice and got the Correctional Centre so hung up believing I dialed wrongly. I have dyslexia so it is quite feasible to error. Finally, I chance asking for the individual by name. The gentleman was a correctional officer and MY number was on file for IF they couldn't get HIS parent. Fuming I was adamant about getting MY number off their files and NO I was not responsible for his well-being and NO he could not be dropped off at my place.!!!

This lady, and I use the term very loosely, was against post-secondary education and I'm proud to say all four of mine have completed post-secondary school. Each are gainfully employed even during Co-vid.

She had called to say Chris was a terrible driver and to not let him use the car. Curious because to me, he was a good driver, but you never know about teens unsupervised.

In my infinite wisdom I asked George to secretly lie in the back of the Taurus Wagon while Chris drove to pick up his friend 20 km away. Being New Year's Eve Chris was stopped in a RIDE program. Cop is shining light on George and asking Chris repeatedly "anyone else in the car?" Chris denies. Finally George sits up and says "I am here". Poor Chris nearly died of shock. Good job he was not driving! Once the cop knew the reason he let the boys drive on with the advice for George to buckle up!!

After the marital separation I took the kids to see a psychologist because they were excelling which is contrary to the text book pattern for separated/divorced kids. He interviewed them together and individually. Apparently with me being the main care giver, nothing was amiss with them. They were more relaxed because no longer were we walking on egg shells not knowing what the mood of Petrus would be when he entered the house. As soon as the truck's wheels sounded in the driveway, everyone tensed. This was no longer happening. Petrus was never an active participant in running the house property so to the kids, everything was the same. I was the only one fretting about finances and coping......

I am so stupid! I know intellectually and know by personal experience, we do marry a person like our dad. I never saw love from my Dad or from my husband. He was detached and attached only to his bio family. WE didn't count.

Poor George had a terrible time in senior Kindergarten. He heard the teacher tell a student to hurry up or he would be left behind. George believed it was true as the kid was there when he left the school and there before him the next morning. He was so worried about food and how he'd manage if that happened to him. I promised I'd come to get him IF this should ever happened, I assured him the kid didn't stay over and never would. It was a serious misunderstanding that warped his perceptions of security.

Lucky for me the family farm had a great hired man. In fact, overall the hired man gave me more physical help with the gardens than my husband ever did. He even helped after the separation. What a good man!

Petrus did take the two youngest camping in the tent trailer with his new wife. She was some upset that Daniel aged 5 got up at 6 a.m. to go to the washroom by himself. She then locked both boys out of the camper for the day. They refused to go with them again. She did a lot of segregation of the kids. If she took drinks out to Petrus, they got nothing. If she BBQ'd steak for Petrus, they got chicken wieners. She would not allow them to choose their towels or food. She made them eat off plates the dogs had licked. One son developed such a phobia of hair on his food that he would not eat at any place but my home. It was so tough for them, so they quit going over to his place.

Being a country bumpkin, I planted a garden the year of the marriage. I had put in potatoes and Petrus's mother planted lettuce between the rows. She was some flustered when I put bug powder on the potatoes! It was my garden after all!

We had a reputation of being different from the paternal side of the family. That was good. We were so much more community focused. I tried to give back as much as I received. I actually won the Good Neighbour Award for my dedication to the community. The kids grew up with a sense of community and giving.

In fact a chap from Brighton, who dealt professionally with the farm, dropped in one day for Tylenol. He had a massive headache and no Tylenol. He said he knew he couldn't ask anyone on the other three farms, but knew he could ask me for help. That was me and how I raised my kids. Knowing I was a struggling single parent, he often had and extra cheese gift basket for us!

It is what it is.

CHAPTER THIRTY-THREE

Until the divorce was final, welfare decided the taxes for 120 acres were to be allocated as my income/payment/ entitlement! Again an organization that is not logical. When I had my back surgery the chap needed some papers to validate my expenses. We were living on 400. a month and I needed help...

The intake worker sat beside the desk, refusing to open the damn desk drawer knowing full well I couldn't bend down after my back surgery. The kids were outside playing. Did common sense ever exist? Imbeciles!!!

Petrus's family believed I would take the money payout after the divorce and run back to "home". I had little support up there. Fact was that my friends had moved on, and the kids were settled here. I didn't want to disturb the kids any more than I had too. So I elected to take the value in property which was minimized in value by them. That was not the ex-laws' plan. They had complete disregard for our belongings. With farm machinery they ran over toys, bikes, even the chain the dog was tied up to. I had to involve the police.

When the surveyor wanted to do the survey for my portion, Petrus demanded the field driveway be his, so the surveyor just added on the amount of land to the back of the property. All is fair in love and war.

It is what it is!!!

Going back home also increased the risk of jeopardizing my kid's safety if my sexual perpetrator should assault them. Now as it so happened, we had a family gathering when my sister grabbed my arm and said, "Look.". There was this brother, full erection, nearly hopping out of his chair as he leered at the triplets. Their bum crack was showing as they squatted over a game on the floor. She raced off to warn the dad. Now this same sister denied vehemently nothing happened to me?????

Decisions were extremely difficult. Never once did my bio family ask how we were managing. Again I felt like a loser. The kids were so instrumental in holding us together. We were a tight-knit family. The lack of food affected two of them immensely. If we had a package of wieners, they each got 2.5 each. I did without. No chicken wieners for us. Yuck!!! The rations kept them conscientious of not wasting food. We made mostly homemade food so it saved money. I feel sad today that they had to experience that.

I don't recollect knowing about food banks or Christmas baskets. One church did provide a basket once when I was strapped. For some reason some folks think it may be offensive to help someone out. I was never that pretentious. Not once do I recall any bio-family asking if I needed help in any way, shape or form. Now the cahp that rented the pig barn did supply pork to us. That helped a lot.It is my conclusion, git certificates are the way to go rather than item donations. That way, one can get what your family will eat and need. There are only so many pastas one can eat.

CHAPTER THIRTY-FOUR

The kids loved their pets. Barkley was a huge Newfoundlander dog that loved his "kids" We had ducks that would wonder over to the neighbors' pond. Usually throwing sticks in the water with Barkley fetching, they meandered out and back home. This one particular night, the ducks were being obstinate so Chris peeled off his shorts and shirt to dive in with only his boxers on. Barkley jumps to alert, and comes out of the water holding Chris's boxers!!!! Poor lad had to run naked back home covering his privates with his hands!!!!

I was rather cautious with the ducks and took the golf club with me just in case. One wee duckling was a straggler. I'd pick him up until mama decides to count. I placed it back on the path for her to okay the attendance. Literally she goes down the row doing a head count! Well last time I quickly deposited him on the ground; he got in the long grass and was no-where to be seen. Frustrated I was swinging the golf club back and forth in the grass. Oh dear- off went his head. I mourned and mama duck mourned. I've never touched a golf club since.

Then some dumbass hunters from Montreal went bang, bang, bang in our field. I counted the shots and thought oh no! that is our ducks!! Confronting them they said the farmer gave them permission to hunt there. Well that was my land so, no I didn't. Should have charged them, but they took off in a hurry. Some were Muscovy ducks, with the tuff on their heads. The kids called them "cool dude!"

To the chagrin of the kid, and unsure of how long it took an egg to hatch we meaning I, decided to check one egg for signs of life. Oh my, there was a partially formed duck, heart beating visibly. Like Humpty Dumpty I couldn't put it back together again. The kids never let me live that one down.

Being new at this nesting business, I thought I was helpful when a duckling was working its way out of the shell, by peeling back the shell. This is before google time, so with its floppy neck I was unsure of what to do. Frantic phone calls to my "google" friend Karen I cupped it in my hands, letting it peck away. The neck grew stronger but the duckling followed me everywhere. Last we saw it was following my car down the road. It never came home. I never helped a hatching bird again!

It is what it is!

Now there was a goose that was extremely protective. My dearest friend Karen would come over, get out of the car, half way to the house, goose would intervene sending Karen back to the car! Poor Dale built an addition on the back of the house so I had access to the basement without going outside. Dale in his eighties still chuckles how the old goose would not let him off the roof nor take breaks. My built in task master. The younger boys dug a water pond in the flower bed to put goldfish in. Made for a tasty snack for the geese! People gave us hens so we had lots of fresh eggs. I take 26 hours for a hen to produce an egg. We had four hens and five people. Each day we had enough eggs for breakfast. God provides. Then our neighbors' dog, a lab started taking our eggs and laying them on the doorstep of their house!

Our senior neighbors' reported how at 6 a.m. dogs, ours and the neighbors, met at the mail box and proceeded down the road for a walk of 45 minutes. They would return, touch noses and part ways again.

One time their son staying overnight on the sofa, awakened to this loud slurping sound outside the window. He peered out, only to see this HUGE back animal drinking out of the rain barrel. Thinking it was a bear he yelled and it simply looked in the window at him. Dear Barkley.

The other neighbor would share how when he came home and went to the mailbox at dark, this big black animal was coming forward: he didn't know whether to run to our place or his own!!! Just Barkley meandering about.

Barkley seemed to know when I was working overnight shifts. Being the breed he was he preferred outside but when I'd leave for the 11-7 shift he wanted in the house. As soon as I came home he was out again. One particular weekend I went to Gracefield Christian Camp/Conference for some recharging of the batteries. That place provided tranquility for me for so many years and still does. I was a camp counsellor there during my teens, attend family camp with the kids, attended One Parent Family Retreat weekends there, organized a Divorced/Separated and their kids workshop there, volunteered there, just treasured it incredibly so. The kids were old enough to manage on their own plus Karen kept an eye out for them as she always did.

The kids walked to church and Barkley went right along. He went into the church as well. It was Communion Sunday. He sniffed around the bread and juice not touching anything before returning to lay behind the pew the kids sat in. Well some fuddy-duddy old ladies thought this was just awful a dog in church, so Maggie drove the dog and Chris back to the house. Before they got back to the church, Barkley was there. He quietly sat through the service and returned home with the kids. That's our Barkley.

When we got him from the Humane Society the paperwork indicated Barkley did not like cats or women. True enough about the cats, if you were between him and a cat, you were in China when you quit spinning. He had no problem with me or any other woman.

Otherwise Barkley was very docile and did not eat copious amounts. A travelling sales man came to sell some pork chops, I said "no thanks," I have barn full of pigs and all the chops I needed. When he insisted these were the best, Barkley growled. The man moved on to Chicken Kiev at an exorbitant price. Told him I could get cheaper and just as good from the local grocery store. Upon his arguing, Barkley growled and the man departed never to return. Otherwise I never heard that dog growl or ever be mean.

When the ice storm moved we had re-located and Simone often went for runs or walks. We were missing her, wondering about her whereabouts, and eventually could see a black form down the side road. I took the car down and there she was- over the back of Barkley. She was soaked from falling in the ditch, and when she collapsed on the road old Barkley got himself under her, hoisting her on his back. He was bringing her home. What a close call. Again Barkley saved her.

As Barkley failed, Simone would return from her runs and would have to take the car to pick the old guy up. It was too much for him, but he remained faithful. It was a sad day that we laid him to rest in our backyard. The memories and love live on. RIP Barkley

It is what it is!

Simone had a pony that was the size of the dog, that could barely lift her feet over a small step. Candy was exceptionally docile until the neighbors had a loud party, and over the fence that creature went. How many trips were there to find Candy munching on a neighbors' yard? A bucket of oats would draw her back into captivity. She'd come to me but not to Petrus. He beat her badly once and she never forgot. Petrus's actions were just awful. She had bucked when one of the kids was on her back, and he beat her until she sat down on her hind haunches. Just terrible and terrifying for all of us. When he split she was more docile.

Sadie was Daniel's dog. Well more accurately Daniel was Sadie's' weakest link. She showed up one night, whining at his window, I took her to the vet's to check for a microchip. I called the dog catcher informing him I had the dog if anyone was looking. He said because the dog was found up here, probably the owner was nearby. Two weeks went by. We bathed that dog because she sure did stink, fed that dog and Daniel was begging to keep her. Apparently an owner in Ottawa gave it to someone in Osgoode who gave hit to someone in Smiths Falls, then back to Osgoode, and finally to our area. I repeatedly went into the vets and they can't give out phone numbers. Somehow the file was left open within my eyesight. I took it upon myself to snag a phone number. 10 o'clock at night I call to find out they don't want the dog. We can keep Sadie.

One particular night after my oldest son returned from work I hear him loudly whispering for Daniel to come quick. I was partially asleep but awake enough to follow what is transpiring. Dear Sadie had opened the door to allow five other dogs into the house. They were eating her food and tearing around the living room. The nerve!

It is what it is.

Surprisingly one day, a police officer comes to the house to "rent" Sadie for hunting. I don't know how to do this- by the day, by pound, how? I deflect saying it is Daniels' dog which it was. Daniel thinks I have lost my marbles until he sees the business card. We agree to rent the dog and the funds received can buy dog food. That dog loved that cop. The cop and his cronies loved Sadie. She gave them good results. Now mind you, if this cop shot a deer absolutely no-one but him could come near while Sadie was on duty.

Another year Sadie disappears on first day of the hunting season. The men are quite worried but return to camp. There was Sadie in one of the sleeping bags, quite comfortable and as if to say, "My day is done." The dog had a habit of crawling inside anything and everything so that sometimes it was difficult to see her.

Then Sadie gets this swollen ear, so I consult the vet. She needs surgery but I maintain it can't happen until after hunting season. A cone around her neck in the bush would not suffice. By golly, a day after she left, the vet calls to say it is not my dog and surgery can't be done. The dog catcher says I have to surrender the dog and could face being charged with kidnapping a dog. Excuse me!!! If I'm going down it will be for something bigger than taking a dog!!! They ask where the dog is. I say "with the police" Grin*

Daniel and I spent hours trying to locate that owner. We did. He agreed he would testify he gave the dog to us. I had forgotten to change the microchip.

It is what it is.

Years passed and eventually Sadie was diagnosed with a huge cancerous growth between her heart and her lungs. I've never had to choose a death date for a pet before. Daniel said he' go and Chris agreed to accompany him for support. They both bawled so much. RIP SADIE

That was the one and only time I had to slate an animal's demise. It was heart-wrenching. I could see in Sadie's eyes that morning she understood there were no other options. I cried- no I bawled all the way to work.

I still can't bring myself to get another dog.

Now we also had a cat. Tigger would wait until Sadie was in the cage for the night, then reach through the bars and swat the dog. That cat knew payback would happen if the dog was loose. That same cat would bat my partner's leg if he was less than swift first thing in the morning to dole out treats. Chris's cat is known for going on walks with us. She toddles along and meows when she has a comment. That cat talks human. I swear she told me a distinct "NO"!

That cat is super sensitive to illness. She wanted on top of my knee replacement knee for weeks, and cuddled up to the grandson (who hates animals) when he had an ear infection! Now she wants on my tummy as I await gall bladder surgery With us the cat is dismissive at the best of times. Somehow they just know!

CHAPTER THIRTY-FIVE

It was quite challenge being a full-time single parent of four kids basically two years apart. Schooling was challenging to say the least. Four wanting homework help simultaneously created stress and chaos in the evenings. Just fathom parent-teacher interviews, to which I always went.

When Chris started school, one night the bus went sailing past the house. His wee face was pressed against the window. I frantically call the school who in turn tried to get hold of the driver. The driver had reached the end of his route with a kid left over. When he was returned I asked him why he didn't say something to the driver. He replied, "You told me not to talk to strangers!" There was a new driver while the regular one went to the plowing match.

Poor wee Daniel had started Junior Kindergarten when the bus arrived amidst a dreadful rainy, windy storm. I ran to get him from the bus and back into the house. We were both cold and drenched to the skin. I told him to go upstairs to change and me, well no-one was around, so I stripped behind the island in the kitchen, when, whoops, the mailman dropped in with a parcel. The only thing I could grab was a magazine for cover. Next time seeing him in the grocery store was embarrassing. I just hadn't made it to the laundry room in time!

Chris had a habit in high school of skipping classes. I was on my way to Morrisburg, 40 km from the school when I noticed two hitchhikers. I turned around and caught up to them. One was my dearly beloved, Chris. They had the nerve to ask for a ride back. I had my dental appointment so no way. Chris came home that night and knew he was grounded. Another time, he was so argumentative in the car in Cornwall I dropped him off despite the snowstorm. He called his friend for a ride and ASKED permission to continue living at home. He did go to Petrus's for 3 days and decided nope he wanted back home.

Last time of skipping was a learning curve for him. I had him pick rocks from a neighbors' field. He had access to the tractor, lunch, water and I checked in at noon. Well he was picking every size of rock. Lawrence had the cleanest field ever. I refused to tell him what size of rocks- the value of education!!!

It is what it is.

Rock picking a farmer's field was heaven for my rock finds, while others scoffed and grumbled about the heat, the work, the attitudes, the crappy lunch or anything they could drum up on short notice. I treasured and delighted in the quarts, mica, and varying geological finds. Take me somewhere in a car, and I am alert for flat unique rocks to bring home. Many made it to my rock garden!

It is what it is.

Now Chris had experienced a teacher in grade 6 that was exclusive of his Independent Learning Recommendations. She purposefully put him in every situation contrary to the recommendations. The other students acknowledged she singled him out and was unfair to him. I moved him out to the Catholic system where he excelled. I on the other hand stayed involved on hot lunch Fridays to purposefully deliver food to her classroom. I witness how she was so disorganized. Bedlam existed. Unions protect slothful, negligent teachers by just transferring them to another school. This needs to change.

When George started high school, teachers asked if Chris was his brother, to whom he replied yes and quickly added Simone was his sister. No need to think behaviors were similar. Daniel had a learning disability and progressive testing was not done because he was too well behaved! .

In Senior Kindergarten, the teacher wanted to put Simone in special education classes. She felt she was "slow". I asked if she had to be asked the second time to do things. No. Well she was well-mannered and having three siblings she knew to take her turn without shoving in line. They "tested" her and her vocabulary was of grade six! Yes I read bedtime stories to each: no we did not repeat rhymes over and over. Today she has her Master's in Occupational Therapy. As a parent you have to be on your toes and fight for your kids. I did- and to think my parents never ever attended a school interview.

Daniel in grade twelve was watching TV instead of studying for exams. He told me he'd study in the morning. Being an early riser, I could see him doing that. BUT in the morning he is watching cartoons. He tells me if he doesn't know the stuff by now it is too late. I head off to work, tense, stressed and frustrated. Down the road I realize I have passed grade 12 and it is his responsibility not mine. He aced it.

Chris was heading off to Humber College but maintained employment right up to seven-thirty of departure day. We had loaded that Taurus wagon the night before so off we went off while he slept. Rats! It was hot and windows were open, when the directions blow out along the 401!!! I stop close to Toronto to buy a map and we winged it. He knew the street but not the number. Up and down the street we meandered looking if there was a sign of rental. Nope. Thankfully this lady came out when we were stopped and inquired if we were looking for her place. That was the address. WHEW! Country bumpkin Chris was hyped to meet real city folks. LOL His roommate was from the rural county his grandparents lived in!!!!

When we stayed at a motel near the airport and walked over to the Waffle House, a cop stopped Chris and told him, he was jaywalking. Chris asked, "What is jay walking"? The cop asked, "Where are you from"? Being from a hick countryside gained Chris some leniency. Each other gave the other a break and we deemed it a learning curve.

At least I never had to hear one of my kid's say to me, as my grandson at age ten, said to his mother-"Go upstairs and eat all your make-up then maybe you will be beautiful on the inside!"

When you think of kids, you think girl or boy. I had a granddaughter staying with me for a week when she was two. I asked her to stay on the deck while Grandma mowed the grass. She complied so when we are in the living room I said, "What a good girl to listen to Grandma!"

The response was, "I am not a girl. I am a boy!" Now I had noticed she stole her younger brother's underwear, shorts and shirts. She also had removed earrings her mother had gotten for her pierced ears and taken the scissors to get short hair. So I say, "But as a girl you can do everything, anything a boy does." She is two! I'm told with hands on the hips for emphasis, "But I am a boy and if you call me a girl again Grandma, I will call you GRANDMOTHER!' Ouch, I had been told!

Three years later I recommend to her dad, better go get a consult with CHEO. Sure enough she is a little boy trapped in a girl's body. Now at the age of twelve there has been no wavering-absolutely no iota of doubt. Everyone who meets this child sees a boy. In a small kiddie pool, of fresh water from the hose, he declares his balls are freezing!'

There was a month of intense grieving on my part. Where did my granddaughter go, and where did this grandson come from? Our agreement is up to the age of two I can say "she" but unless I want a charlie horse, it had better be "he"! Figuring my much older brother in his eighties would struggle the hardest with this change: he simply cocked his head saying, "all we can do is love the child."

He has chosen his own name. His mom is dallying on making the changes to identification. That worries me. If the child is in an accident and the medical personnel are calling the female name: he won't respond. Statistics indicate 95% commit suicide because of a lack of family support. We have your back kiddo!

My fear is someone will beat him up just because they are close minded. This book title is his favorite expression.

Uncle Chris is so supportive of the kids. They adore him. Chris has had his share of experiences in life.

When Chris was learning to drive, he literally took my directive. The day of the test, he asked which way to go. I told him straight through. Well he went through the stop sign, I panicked. He said, "Well you said, straight through!" Now I am explicit with anyone driving. The other rule is to follow my hands not my mouth!

It is what it is!

CHAPTER THIRTY-SIX

Life in our present location is eventful to say the least. Animals like skunks and raccoons felt living under the house was a wonderful housing opportunity. I became quite the trapper.

First time I took a skunk down the road three miles on the cart behind the garden tractor. I knew enough to cover the trap. Wasn't so sure about the laws of re-location though. I passed a car which soon backed up and I was sure I was in trouble. Come to discover I had lost a wheel off the cart and they were bringing it to me. Now I know I also need to go MUCH further from home to do a relocation. Sometimes I ponder painting their stripe so I know if it is the same one returning..

A neighbor called me about a creature in the sandbox. I went out on the deck to shout at this overgrown feral cat. He leaped/hopped and ran closer under the deck. Strange behaviors. I laid the trap. Caught the rascal. It was so heavy to lift and the brat would run from end to end. I would scream and drop the cage.

I figured I would get my Ottawa friend take this feral cat to the Humane Society. It is so ferocious, I decide I can't drive it into Ottawa. So I meander through the back roads before choosing a place to re-home this guy. I let it out and it takes off like a flash. I'm thinking the damn thing will be home before me because I was no longer sure where I was.

Two days later I'm sharing my experience with a dear friend. Samure tells me it is a fisher by my description. WHAT? Looking up on the internet confirms her theory. Those things are ferocious, large, heavy and definitely feral. I'm blessed it didn't attack me. Can you imagine if I took it to the Humane Society and others were as naive as me?

It is what it is.

Reminds me of the time, Jim-bob came over to the house to rescue me. I had come in from the barn to see a bat flying nonchalantly over the kids' heads in the kitchen as they peruse the Sears Christmas catalogue. I have a huge fear of bats. I eventually got their attention by rapping on the window and directed them to call Jim-bob for help. The removal accomplished, he goes to leave and says "what a nice Kitty" to the pile of fluff at the food dish outside. I correct him-"that's a skunk". He bolts back inside. We are unsure how to tell his wife he may be staying overnight!!!

At this new place we raised meat chickens. That worked great until we took them to the butcher. Somehow I recall the rooster being first to go! We waited three months to dissociate before making them supper.

This new place is going to do me in. Folks who should have, could have, would have, did not, leaving me with a lemon. The house is brown so I guess I got a rotten lemon.

Too many professional people were negligent on their job. Only after the purchase did I find out that instead of a bungalow it was a trailer with additions, many additions of which none were done to code nor even had a building permit for.

I followed the recommendations of hiring a building inspector but got screwed in the end. Had the lawyer researched as he should have, I would not be in this mess. The owners had lied about the age, knocking off 15 years so everyone assumed everything was completed to code. As we learn – assume means ass -U and me.

To fight this I needed a $25,000 retainer fee as it was a multi-person lawsuit which I did not have. The home inspector says "I didn't fall thru the roof" so it must be good. I'm not Homer Simpson either! When I finally got nerve to climb to the roof, I could see the uneven shingles at the edges. I curse the previous owner. As time progresses, more and more defects are discovered.

I had additional kitchen cabinets put in. The poor installer said studs were a variety of inches apart instead of the mandatory 16 inches. I do love my cabinets.

My son did some room Reno to find a brown towel by the light fixture. Why??? Another socket in the foyer was shorting out. I could not identify the ticking sound. Fortunately Chris identified and fixed the problems. Too many things were on that fuse. We could have had a fire.

The guy also cut corners on the bathroom. Just a side note this chap was a teacher's aide for shop class!!!! The vent for the bathroom was simply vented to the attic, not outside. The house/trailer is leaning to the west. The trailer is not on a foundation. Where do I get affordable help?

I did qualify for a forgivable loan that enabled me to get new windows and doors. Would you believe my previous patio doors were secured only by insulating foam? Doorways had no supporting boards and yes the lean was obvious. The

IT IS WHAT IT IS

installers were a fantastic crew installing in February. On Valentine's Day I treated them to pizza. All agreed it was the best pizza they had ever had- all but one guy. That guy had just spent three days boasting how he had the biggest window, highest job to do, widest door and so on. Well I went and got him a pin. "What is that for?" he asked. "Poke yourself- let all your hot air out", I replied. He had irked me beyond my limits! The big boss quietly says, "I knew someone would get him someday: I didn't expect it to be you!"

My shingles were getting past their prime. But a storm made short work of patches. Insurance felt they would not cover the damage due to age of the shingles, but an answer to prayer eventually they did. I got a wonderful new roof, new skylights and a new valley. Two weeks later in another storm, a tree crashes onto the new roof! Come on, enough is enough! Thank God the boys were able to fix the damage and another claim did not have to be processed

It is what it is.

During this time, I also take the palliative care course. Jokingly I tell people, I can bring you into the world (midwife) and take you out (palliative care) and everything in between, so do not mess with me!

I am assigned to this young chap who has Muscular Dystrophy. He is sharing about this young gal he met in high school and has lost track of. Yikkers- he is talking about my daughter. Of course the professional route is not to disclose about our family so I check with the Co-coordinator what to do. The parents authorize a connection. Young Willy is ecstatic to connect with Simone. He wants me to write love notes from his dictation. Excuse me I can't write that!!!! He speaks of marrying her and elaborates on the wedding details. He makes his parents promise when/if something happens to him that they will take care of her.

Unfortunately, he passes suddenly and all our hearts are crushed. He promised he'd be an angel looking out for us. When we come home from the hospital, the angel on the tree is sitting at an angle it can't logically maintain without falling.

When there are bad storms, a white light circles our rooms. I was to buy a particular bottle for Simone to put a poem in, and it takes three tries. It breaks twice before I get it home. The day he passed the glass on the china cabinet cracks. Simone is devastated. Her heart feels like it is breaking in half.

Now I feel I made a huge mistake in letting Simone continue on being involved with his parents. He had no siblings. They take over as parents. Financially they can provide for her better than me. I feel left out and negated. They follow her wherever she is going to school.

Have they taken their promise to extremes?

My heart is broken.

CHAPTER THIRTY-SEVEN

How and when did my life unfold or unravel? Was it sudden or progressive? Maybe my life was never "together" from day one? To the doctor I didn't exist. I was menopause. I am resilient. I'm not infallible. I'm not done being mad yet and I am not bullet proof.

When my first granddaughter turned two, I had a mental collapse. I was working as an addictions counsellor when all the memories came flooding back. Didn't help I suffered from Season Affective Disorder (SAD). Neither I nor my supervisor recognized it. This is deplorable for an agency that theoretically specialized in mental health and addictions.

I had great performance reviews in the fall but when the reviews were changed to late Feb I was so discontent. I was told I was a "product of my own creation". Meaning I took the parent program from 1x a week to two groups running a week with double the attendees. The success rating as 10/10. I had a client list of 95 to every other counsellor's 12-25. I was also sent into a school to work on top of my workload simply because I was experienced!

So when Annabelle was born I was burnt out, and suffering from PTSD.

I couldn't fathom how someone could allow a two year old to be sexually abused. To me it I felt like the abuse always happened and for forever. My mother finally confessed to an older sibling that she caught my brother sexually assaulting me when I was 2 years of age.

I knew then why I tied the door shut.

I recoil remembering how I felt squished- I can't breathe and oh my God he stank. No wonder I developed hemorrhoids at such a young age and still have today as a token reminder. The vaginal infections made sense.

There was a particular morning where I was to wear these brown polyester pants to school but there was white stuff on them. My mom washed it off. Now I know it was sperm!

He often would not shave, so someone who has a mustache, unshaven face and has coffee breathe sends me into a tailspin. My stomach tightens, my heart speeds up and I break out in a sweat. PTSD in full bloom.

My mom warned me once to just stay away from him. But he followed me everywhere. In the woodshed, he asked if I wanted a baby. I said yes. After all, my nieces and nephews were pretty darn sweet. Then he said we have to do it like the cows and bull did it. I had no idea. ?????

My mom excused his behavior because he was retarded/ mentally challenged- whatever term you want to apply. Don't get your knickers in a knot over the term- look at what he did.

As an early teen we cut cedar brush to make money, tying up the bales with baler twine. Many times my younger bro Allan had to help with other farm chores, so I was left to do the brush alone. I'd be snipping along when I'd hear a branch break- scared it was a bear, I'd make more noise singing, more footsteps- that drag from one leg to the other one leg. Damn- what do I do? He would grab me and assault me.

My mom admitted to my older sister that many times she found me crying and I wouldn't say why. Now bear in mind this man is 12 years older than me and stronger than an ox. No –one ever chose to get him riled up. Why??? Why did I not speak up? To whom??? He threatened to kill me if I said anything. I had nightmares, always dreaming of escape plans. I wanted to run away. Sometimes I did – back to the bush. Once I took the centre out of the woodpile for the sugar camp, made myself a little cubbyhole and stocked it with apples, carrots and other garden supplies and books. I'd spend the day hiding out till after dark. No-one enquired where I had been. I was deemed the troubled emotional teen.

Only now I know that my older siblings see him as the whistling blonde haired kid who got very sick when he was 4/5. They can't visualize what he did to me. When someone speaks well of him, I cringe in sadness. What they don't know.

Finally when my mom went on a trip overseas with her sister I had to milk the cows in her stead. The cows hated my dad and rightfully so. He was mean to them. This jackass bro followed me to the barn and attempted to have sex with me. Having enough of everything, I took a 2x4 to him. Wow did I get a licken' from my dad for that! Not that he even asked why I had beaten him. That stopped a lot of the attempts but he was still subtle in being sexual.

Doing the mealtimes dishes in the summer kitchen while my parents napped he would try to pass between the sideboard and the table stopping to dry hump me as he squeezed though. He even felt my son Chris was his child. Now doesn't that speak volumes?

It wasn't until I was in post-secondary school in Toronto that I read in her diary, she had gotten help for my disabled brother's sexual behavior. This was sparked because he touched her knee one evening ^$ %*(*)!! Excuse me!!! He only touched your knee?????

What was I? Garbage? A Lost cause? What I felt and internalized was not conducive to confidence or positive self-esteem.

CHAPTER THIRTY-EIGHT

After many years of counselling I came to a deeper understanding of what probably transpired... Apparently my dad wanted to put him in an institution and my mom wanted to keep him at home. Technically, he never progressed past an age of 5 or so. The other aspect was his disability cheque was money for my mom. Probably the only money she had access to other than the child tax benefits. Anger prevails for all of us from different sources.

Anger is an interesting emotion. Anger is a perfectly normal emotion as long as it is expressed appropriately. Unfortunately it is often a destructive display so gets a bad rap. It is interesting and challenging to know that behind anger is one of two emotions or perhaps a combination thereof, hurt or fear. It is difficult to distinguish what you are truly afraid of or hurt by.

I'm angry I was sexually assaulted because I was afraid of dying during the process. I was also hurt that no-one appeared to value my well-being or my safety. Knowing that helps to place the event safely in the recesses of my mind. I am not scott free by any means. Now I know anger still scares me. I related it to being physically hurt or sent away. Yes I am very insecure. I remain fragile-very fragile.

After being involved with the Sexual Assault counselling group I took my then boyfriend up to confront my brother where he resided in a nursing home. He confessed he knew what he had done to me, and that he felt it was his "job" when my mom told him to look after me. I knew beyond certain he was more accountable than I was led to believe. The devious, planned, and intentional acts were his conscious doing.

I don't know why, when my parents fought, I was sent to my other sister's in the middle of the night. Was it for my protection against my dad's wrath?? I recall hearing him shouting, I peeked down through the chimney pipes in time to see him slap her across the face. The door slammed, I scooted back into bed then my oldest bro was there to take me to my sister's. Why just me? My younger brother was there. I heard discussion around my Dad's returning from wherever he disappeared to, but the rest is blank. Probably I spent a couple of days at my sisters. No discussion then, after, or even now.

CHAPTER THIRTY-NINE

I lacked emotional support in my career. Working in the mental health and addictions field was tedious and general void of feel good moments anyways. I was so elated when I received this message from a client:

"I understand that you personally did not have a good experience with certain people in that organization and for that I hold you higher than my arms will allow, such that God knows you and your beauty. You see good in whatever is laid before you. You immerse yourself without concern.

As a Christian, you shine brightly - a North star. Never forgetting who we love - you are so near and dear to me because you're as pure a Christian as they come.

Really love and admire you!

Wish the world was wall to wall full of Maria's."

Now that client was high profile in the city and did not want his identity known or the fact his child was into drugs. He only gave minimal information on intake. Being a parent without his child involved he became my client. Poor chap nearly passed out at first meeting. He put a different name and date on his "forms' so I just kept changing datis. Took some flak from my supervisor but that was small potatoes to me, my goal was to genuinely help people, not be a paper pusher! First group attendance I wasn't even sure he was well enough to drive home-wherever that was. He kept changing that info as well. By the end of 10 weeks he was willing to be a spokesperson for the agency!!!

He and I bonded in a very special way. Not only was he handsome, he was a Christian! Now in an agency you are not to share your beliefs but I still let my little light shine in small overt ways. Christians would single me out and say "you are a believer- aren't you?" I trust God will also hold me high in the judgement days.

Other clients were something else. In one particular class (20 folks present) I was doing an illustration. My point was to divide the group and have them problem solve. One lady took me literally in her role as the injured soul and plunked herself on the floor. Busy teaching I didn't see nor hear her, so when I stepped backwards I nearly went as-over-tea kettle. She was a hoot but often had to be reined in. Sharing an event she would describe in minute detail- "I got yellow curtains with white polka dots. Polka dots were varying sizes but scattered over the fabric and on and on and on". Point was her kid had sold his guitar for drug money!! I'd have her write out the things she wanted to share and condense the key points! Ten minutes per parent didn't allow for details!

That place got to me. Management got to me, not the clients. I have little tolerance for political nonsense and absence of a direct answer. Deceit kills me.

So many clients were special to me. I admired their tenacity. One young lad, only known to me through word of mouth from the multi-cultural liaison worker was on the bridge to Hull, ready to jump in. I was summoned. His "stuff" had already been thrown in yet he agreed to speak with me before he jumped. Talk about fervent prayer. He came back to the office with me. When I found out he took such a risk to come with me I was in awe. He figured he was going to die one way or another. True enough- no-one gets out of life alive.

Well he had been caged in Somali for smoking pot, and he watched people kill each other for food. Sanitary conditions were non-existent. You publically went to the bathroom in a corner of this chicken wire cage. It had a tin roof. He figured I may cage him up, yet he risked coming with me. I got him some food and we talked and talked, and talked. He was illiterate in written English but fluent in six other languages. He kept my business card in his shoe and matched the numbers to call me every day for check in from the homeless shelter. We had to start from scratch getting identification so he could go to a treatment centre for drug use. Do you know with no identification, it is like you don't exist? You need to have this to get that scenario. We persevered. I had him all lined up for a treatment centre when I had an accident at home leaving me unable to go to work. He bolted in fear.

Stupid does what stupid does. I had March break off and happy I had also taken the Monday off so I could relax with zero kids. Returning from the bathroom in the night, with no lights on, I flopped onto the bed thinking, "Yes, no kids!" Whoops I forgot I had moved my bed to the far side of the room. I crashed- LOUDLY. An ambulance was called. I already had stenosis of the upper spine so further swelling, bruising and torn ligaments were not what I needed, but what I got. How do you explain a fall like that?

Everyone kept asking, "How much did you have to drink?" NOTHING. To this day no-one lets me forget and I've never moved my bed since!

So this young chap and I played tag a lot. I have a residential centre but I don't have him. I have him but no centre space available. I've been called to get him out of jail. Those bars really clang like the movies!

He doesn't know why he was picked up. He was out past his curfew which he didn't know because he can't read. The jail guard hands me the paperwork telling me to explain the conditions. I tell him that is his job and that the young man does not read English. The lad disappears again and I expect he is messed up with the drug lords in Montreal. I close his file. Bingo! He shows up. I pinch him to see if he is real! So eventually we get everything together and he is slated to go to Dianova in Quebec.

I have to take him shopping for clothes to take with him on a hundred dollars from Social Services. I estimate costs as we shop at Giant Tiger. He needs underwear. I ask him what size and he starts to pull down his pants for me to check. Whoa buddy! not in a store and not on my time!!! At the cash he asks if there is enough money to buy a disposable camera- there is.

I get him McDonald's for the bus and then he says, "Can I tell you something?" Apprehensively I say "okay spill." He says "I don't want to go!" Really you got to be jostling me. Then he laughs and hops on the bus. Incidentally, this kid had used so much of everything the night before he should be dead. A garbage can junkie. This means he did not have a drug of choice: anything would do.

Cutting the story short, I received a letter in English, thanking me and how he wants to emulate me in the future. Today he runs a huge oil field project. I am so proud of him!!!

I have to share about another sweetheart. He was living with Hell's Angels after a CAS placement went sour. His bio mom had passed and his siblings were spread apart. Now this lad had dreadlocks and reeked so much of pot, I was high after an hour appointment in my window-less office.

I showed the video **_Basketball Diaries_** in two parts just before Easter to the group of ten students. I was trying to motivate this group to reducing/stopping their drug use. This lad wanted to be Prime Minister letting pot flow freely. At the conclusion of the movie which I was hoping would help them define where their bottom "line" of conscience was, I handed out those small Easter eggs you buy in a mesh bag for ninety-nine cents. He was last out of the classroom, and he remarked, "Miss I haven't had an Easter egg since my mom died." Well then, I gave him the rest.

Tuesday he returns to school, looking terrible. I ask what is wrong?- figuring he tried something different with negative results. He says, "Miss I went cold-turkey and stopped everything." I'm asking why? I didn't see this coming! He said if I cared enough to give him an Easter egg then he needed to take care of himself. He graduated top of his parenting class!!!! My sweet man.

It is what it is.

Being a multi-cultural school there was often language or cultural hurdles. A Muslim girl raped by her own dad is using marijuana to cover up the emotional pain. I don't blame her. Of course being Muslim, the rape is bad enough, but we also had to scurry to find money for an abortion. Now in Ottawa, the assumption would be she returned to her native country, and in that country the assumption is that she is in Ottawa. Honor killings were prevalent and acceptable. Through court, we got her a Canadian Citizenship and all continues well. Again understandable there are some mental health issues.

It would appear that those who have been sexually abused, have mental health problems, but all with mental health problems have not necessarily sexually abused

Another young man was a total card. To remain in school and in conjunction with probation orders, he was to see me. So every appointment he comes in refusing to speak because he is only mandated to "see me." This continues with me keeping him the full hour. There are drug use posters on the wall and lots of booklets to browse. He does. Once in a while, he asks a question. All I find out is he loves blueberry pie and has new running shoes. He wants me to write a letter to probation services as the semester draws to a close, indicating he completed the mandate. No way! I tell him it would be unprofessional to accredit him with change when he did not even engage. Time goes on and slowly he opens up. I refer to him as my nut. I know there is goodness within but his shell is hard to crack- like a Brazil nut. I am no longer in that school and lo and behold he seeks me out in the new agency. My special little nut has opened his shell!

For some, being pregnant was the changing point of stopping drug use to keep baby healthy. You would be astounded at the variance of drug use and how these young ladies stopped cold turkey. You can't predict a bottom line.

So there were many good times and so many tears in this field. It is called Vicarious Trauma when you experience the client's struggles through working with them. It contributes to burnout. The parents and kids were precious to me. Thanks be to God for keeping my own kids safe during their adolescent years. Mind you I had "contracts" set up with them, and now have the same contracts with my grandkids. No alcohol, no drugs, no tobacco and no sex and starting at 13 you get fifty dollars, doubling at sixteen, again at eighteen and twenty-one. I need to have trust. If there is an iota of doubt, the deal is off. I don't think anyone of mine made it past eighteen. Now my first granddaughter just collected her fifty. It is incentive to stay clean.

Now going back to the burnout, most of mine was a result of staff, management and red tape.

The younger counselor, especially one led the pack in isolating me. I was her nemesis or vice versa. I had issues with her featuring a Facebook picture of a table ladened with beer bottles when she was an addictions counsellor. Image control is important on social media. The breaking of boundaries when you are serving as a preceptor is not cool. For example she went to the hospital emergency where a student was ill to verify she was indeed ill after the dad called in that was where his daughter was. The doctor had to ask her to leave. I still struggle with counsellors that smoke and smoke with clients. Smoking is an addiction. Role modelling is vital.

I didn't think it was appropriate for the agency to enter a "team" into the cancer walk and proceed to drink heavily there. Two went off on a sexual tryst in the bushes. Time spend organizing was on company time when it really wasn't an agency event?

Another counsellor was sexually flaunting her promiscuous ways. She actually stalked her ex-boyfriend.

Another would only speak French in front of me knowing I don't speak French. Another openly mocked Christianity. All this had a name.

Bullying in the workplace.

I had such a heavy workload and esp. in relationship to the others.

I had taken a grown a parent program to double its size and frequency. It was not my doing to name one group, the 2-4 group. That mean they met on the 2nd and 4th Wednesday! On a fifth Wednesday we would practice self-care and go to a local buffet. That was so much fun at low prices!

I had one prim and proper lady, very articulate and I was so impressed with her composure. I sent notices to get attendance numbers for support meetings- I asked if she were attending- she types back: "Hell yes"! I'm flabbergasted. Good old computers it was a typo – the "o" was left off the hello!

I'm not good with names esp. some that are foreign to me. Take Siohban- how is that Chavon???? Genevieve became Jenny. Well, I need to clarify, even with my own kids I would go through each of their names, and throw the dog's name in before I got the right kid with right name!. Can't provide examples due to confidentiality but they and half the groups know how I fumbled, stumbled, improvised and kept motoring.

We had a relaxation exercise and by gosh I put one man so deep asleep he snored. His poor wife was as embarrassed as we tried to wake him up!!! I ran a tight ship stayed on budget and rated 10/10 on satisfaction reviews.

I was very effective as a clinician. I was highly successful professional, and yes even asked to speak to large groups about our services. This all took a toll on me, emotionally, physically, and psychologically. Thanks to Ally-son for stabilizing me many, many times. She was the best of the best

There was some trying moments. Like the night before class the kitchen went on fire. In advertently my colleague had used a tea towel instead of an oven mitt. She was unaware it had ignited and simply threw it on the counter before going down a floor to her office. This weird gong sound is so loud. I use the PA to ask what it is? Then I saw and smelt the smoke. I call the fire dept. who asks if I am still in the building. Yup I am! Before exiting the building, I take the fire extinguisher aiming for the base of the fire. Thank goodness for the fire extinguisher training years ago. I get it out but smoke and chemicals are so strong. I grab my phone, agenda, purse and exit. True to form the firefighters were hunks!

The cabinets and some counter items need to be replaced. It could have been worse. I was commended for a fast and efficient response.

Two weeks later I ask everyone at the staff meeting to be silent. I can hear water dripping. Seems our supervisor watered an artificial plant over the TV. I spring into action again. My diversity matters.

I burnt out after fifteen years. The norm was to last ten years. I ran a tight ship with my professional life and life as a single parent of four. Relaxation and self-care were basically non-existent. It was a struggle to learn to sit and do nothing. I had to learn to enjoy the nature around me. Purchasing a swing for the deck was very therapeutic.

CHAPTER FORTY

Speaking of ships. I went on a cruise to the Caribbean-first time ever on a cruise. I am not a water person. I love looking at water, but can't swim. I am petrified of being in water.

Now that was partly due to a joke backfiring. At a 4-H meeting I thought it would be funny to topple someone in the lake. Well, with cords on, and full-length coat I went in instead! I bobbed up hitting my head on the dock. They couldn't find me. Finally they located me. I had to be revived.

Now given that scenario, I still chose to be baptized by complete immersion!!! Faith is a powerful thing!!!!

This cruise was going to be a challenge. I was desperately afraid I would be sea sick for the duration. I survived well despite the fourteen foot waves! Let's clarify after the arrival on the ship I was so-o-o sick. Desperately sick at both ends. Three days into this mess, I went to the medical centre for help. Nurse asked if I just used the washroom in the cabin. Heck- no I listed all the places then said one men's washroom on such and such a floor. She nearly dies- "You used a men's washroom?

"Affirmative".

When you have to go, you have to go!

I was quarantined for five of the 10 days! That was horrible. The fifth day I was so bored, I thought I could do some housekeeping. I would change the pictures around. That idea was squashed when I realized the pictures were bolted to the wall. So I asked what the penalties were if I left the room. They said they would fine me. I thought they said find me so yes on a ship there is only so many places to go, that was quite plausible. When I learned the word was fines and that fines were like $2500 dollars, I elected to stay cabin bound.

The young Philippine cabin steward was such a gem to take care of me. He was so accommodating and non-judgmental. I loved him. I wanted to bring him home with me. I'd go again, meaning I'd go on a cruise again.

Wow I also was very fortunate in that I won the local hockey 50/50 draw the week before I sailed. It paid for the trip. One and only time I bought a ticket to boot!

Another de-stressor for me is airplanes. I am very excited by airplanes. I'm amazed at how something so tiny in the sky is actually so big up on the ground. It actually can hold many people. I love landings and take off so I was in my glory every time I had a business trip out west, but just-in-case I had my seatbelt on and a prayer on my tongue.

My daughter introduced me to Cessna introductory flight lessons. I took quite a few of those introductory lessons. I am amazed at how disorganized, stressed, and the general malaise that exists on land and once in the air, things are laid out so neat and orderly. It is a huge stress release for me to get high in the sky. If I had the money I would love to learn to fly.

Had a chap that worked on the runways as a friend. He shakes his head at my obsession.

I am blessed with some VERY close friends that have supported me through thick and thin. They alone were the reason I survived maybe even flourished at times. Ted was a very unique friend. One day the phone rang and it was a wrong number. But the chap says, "You sound nice, is it okay to chat with you?" I agreed and he discussed his confusing love life. He had girlfriend A, B and C (his labels!) and was unsure of how he was going to proceed. I never had that problem with guys, so was intrigued. At the end of the chat he asked for my phone number. Forgetting it was a wrong number, I was perplexed, after all, he called me, then it dawned on me. Okay not to sweat, I gave him the number. He called on a regular basis, helping me through my challenges as well as updating me on his complicated love life. We lost touch but thanks Ted, I hope things worked out for you!

Throughout all these journeys I had medical issues. Being sent for a scan involving fish dye- I coded blue. Previously I would eat fish sticks and even have a craving for a salmon sandwich so I never considered an allergy. Well as soon as they injected that dye, I felt nauseous and the rest is history. The nurse told me about the code blue. It took a long time to stabilize me. No more fish for me. The tiniest piece of tuna in a pasta salad burns my face. For safety's sake I bypass pasta salads in public.

CHAPTER FORTY-ONE

Recently I was having a manic depressive episode when I reached out to Canadian Mental Health after talking to the Crisis line. I wanted to die- no pain, just a sure fired way and quickly. I don't want to be a vegetable from a failed attempt. I didn't have a concrete plan so they figured it is okay to make a referral to Canadian Mental Health.

The intake worker was enough to make me want to end my life with the list of things she gave me to do- file with Criminal Compensation Board for the historical sexual abuse, come to town (50 km away) to join the Monday group for support, check in with family doc, blah, blah, blah.

She overwhelmed me.

I knew and know one of my triggers is pain and the other is fatigue. At this particular time my family doctor was on holidays. My knees are in such terrible pain. I need a cortisone shot. I can't get one through any other avenue. I hate pain. I can't cope with pain. Pain makes me want to die.

The arthritis in both knees was so sore, I could barely walk. My doctor keeps reminding me how lucky I am with the genetics. After all, my grandpa was in a wheel chair in his 40's and my aunt on the other side of the family was badly crippled when she was in her 30's. Cortisone shots work great for me but this time I was left in torture waiting for the doctor's return. Accumulative pain results in no sleep and down I go. Let me tell you Dr. Metcalfe is the best, most awesome person to get cortisone shots from.

Paranoid the first time from horror stories of how the shot hurts, I braced myself for the inevitable. He zooms in with his wheelie stool with my foot on his upper thigh. Then as he moves closer, I say, "Just a minute- do you have your jock strap on?" He asks "why" to which I say, "Look where my foot is and the size of that needle". I didn't want to be responsible for the destruction of his family jewels when I kicked in response to the needle!!! He laughs.

Feeling the instructions from the Canadian Mental Health intake worker HAD to be done I commenced the paperwork for Criminal Compensation Board. Apparently I also need the copies of any reports and notes from professionals involved. Co-incidentally the previous Canadian Mental Health worker had retired, so the agency said they had no records! Excuse me- you are the folks that said I had to do this step and you of all people are failing to supply a letter of support! I'm indignant. I'm in crisis mode and you give me all these things to do!!!! You can't fix stupid even with duct tape!!

Fortunately I had Stefan to guide me through and "find" such letters. The Sexual Assault Team in Ottawa could only write that yes I had attended the support groups. How did I eventually become involved with them???? Who else did I see?

I put together the report for the Criminal Compensation Board as directed. The Board member calls to tell me they got the report but it is disjointed and a trial date will be set. What do they expect when my head is disjointed??? Does no one hear me?? If you hear me, do you understand how getting out of bed is a HUGE task????

During a manic state of depression, I can barely get out of bed. It is work to answer the phone, so I don't. I don't return your calls. I can't. When in that depressive mode I stay in bed, maybe sleeping, maybe just vegging. I can't read............... and either I over- eat or don't eat. I feel totally beyond miserable emotionally. The feelings are ladened with heaviness. It is not that incidents stay in my mind and I stew. No the head is blank, the heart physically aches. I can't identify the sources of pain. Of course not: it is a chemical imbalance. Melatonin, serotonin, and dopamine: they are out of kilter. I am not a scientist.

Sometimes you just go with the flow for today. Today is all you have. Yesterday is past and tomorrow never comes. Time is your answer in conjuncture with the right meds and when that balance is achieved, counselling has its role.

This time the Mental Health Worker can come to the house. Preparation of all the documents for the Victim's Compensation Board was tedious, and naturally the policy was not to keep records or the said professional had moved on. So a trial date was set. My worker Stefan, was not sure he could accompany me because we were going to another city outside of his jurisdiction. I launch a complaint with the director, his boss. The irony and ludicrous policies of agencies asking us to do certain tasks then negating their active involvement befuddles me. That truly annoyed me.

I had my good friend Tish to accompany me. Stefan was eventually allowed to attend. It tore at my gut, my head ached and my heart beat erratically, even though I constantly prayed. I had to take a break halfway through the trial. Somehow, by the grace of God, I made it through. The

Victim Criminal Compensation Board granted me a lump sum payment. That was overwhelming.

I was just so glad they didn't negate what I had experienced all my life! They validate what I had endured was so very, very wrong!!!! Had they negated me, that would have killed me.

That brother had passed on so that was a huge relief for me. I didn't attend the funeral. I always said I wanted to piss on his grave. When I was to the graveyard, I saw his grave. Even the grass hadn't grown there. I felt nothing. I moved on.

Having the home visits by the Mental Health Worker, were especially appreciative since I ended up with total knee replacement on my left knee. It was bone rubbing on bone. Even that surgery didn't go smoothly. First day of the surgery day, I have a sore throat, the outside of my throat, not the inside. The second day I was bruised badly from ear to ear. What is transpiring? Did they shove the artificial knee down my throat?

The story is that during the surgery which was with an epidural, I appeared to be in pain so they gave me a shot of fentanyl. I flat-lined. They were very aggressive in resuscitation. Therefore I had a huge bruise. I recalled at a time during the surgery of hearing the sounds of a hammer and saw. I thought I was in a workshop then it dawned on me that was my knee. Is that when this transpired?

Three days later I get to come home. The nurse wheeling me out the door misjudges distance sending my operated leg into the doorframe. The words I uttered cannot be printed. At home I get down to my bedroom with the walker but it won't fit between the bed and the dresser. I neatly slither off the bed on to the floor, the rest is history. Chris has to call the neighbor for help.

Second night, I am off to bed, when Chris sees me crawling- yes *crawling on my knees* looking for yellow rabbits. I need to get them all and report to the supervisor. The entire event is obscure to me. Again the neighbor is called.

Next day I am trying to find a comfortable place in the living room to sit. I choose the relining rocker. Works great until I have to get up to go to the bathroom. Again the neighbor is called for help. It took a long time to get that knee into a functional state. I know the other one has to be done but it will be a long-long time before I take that journey. The lady who takes my blood samples says she would have twenty kids before she would have that operation again.

This is not the time for people to question me. Having lost control of my kidneys during who knew surgery meant wearing adult diapers. I can't get the stiff operative leg in first so call on my thirty- something son. He is muttering. "I'm not putting diapers on my mom." I tell him this is the beginning and they won't all be clean. He helped. With time I regained continence control.

It is what it is!

As long as the cortisone shots are effective, that will be my action plan. Now be aware that it isn't instant relief. In fact for at least 48 hrs. following the shot the site still hurts just from the injection plus the inflammation. This recent shot remained quite troublesome so I asked my son if he could help me put fresh sheets on my bed that night. Of course I get the spiel if I had used Sunday as my laundry day he was at home to help and so on. Then he says why tonight? I tell him, "'Cause I shit the bed last night not Saturday night!!!!"

Add to this, I also had my diabetic shot of Ozepic which leaves me with a headache and dizziness for 12 hours or so. I also had blood work done. Well I bled something awful from the needle site, drenching my shirt sleeve and dripping like a flowing river. Apparently excessive bleeding is a short-term side effect of cortisone. I did not know!

It is what it is.

You also need to understand that I have an Essential Tremor that has re-shaped my life. Why it is called essential is beyond my comprehension. The brain is malfunctioning and the simplest things are difficult. Try drinking a cup of coffee, writing your name, any actions by the hand and you shake uncontrollably. It varies from a small shake to a grand mal. Somedays I can't even make the instant coffee. The spoon shakes so much all the grinds are off the spoon before I get it out of the jar. Eating out becomes an embarrassment. I need a bib since I wear at least half of what I try to eat. Communion at church is so hard. I struggle to pick up the piece of bread and yes, of course, I spill the wine. Getting zippers lined up and zipped is a challenge as well. I hate to go out with friends because my hands are so unsteady.

Having IBS- Irritable Bowel Syndrome makes outings unpredictable. One day racing home to get to the bathroom in time, I hurried into the foyer washroom just as the bowels released. Thinking I made it just-in-time, I quickly realized the toilet lid was down. Now who leaves the DAMN lid down in my house!!!!!!!!

In life you have to persevere. Answers do not come easily. I was on metformin for 6 months before it was identified as the reason for my fourteen bowel movements a day regime.

Most metformin users have slight bowel problems but for diabetics there are other options. Fight for YOU!!!

Add all these physical problems to a myriad of problems; life can be overwhelming but.....Some will believe my faith is questionable. If God is so real, then why so many problems in my life? God never promised us an easy life but did promise to accompany us throughout the journey. Think of where I'd be if I wasn't spared. DEAD. Look at how I helped others through empathy and intense listening. Let me share one of my son's experiences.

George was driving a set of trains (transport term) on the 401 near Toronto on a stormy wintery day. A car with three little kids in the back seat pulled out in front of him as they left a truck stop. He could see the whites of their eyes, wide with fear. He knew it was going to be a fatality. He says Jesus took the wheel. He managed to get over into the next lane and not end up in the ditch. He saved their lives at the mercy of God. He got a phone call from his boss complimenting him on his driving. Who called in? Who witnessed this? How did they call so quickly? Jesus saves whether you believe or not.

It is what it is.....

Through all these years I have been plagued with bad dreams or nightmares. Essentially I am trying to escape and find safety. I know the reasons, I know the coping techniques yet they continually happen. Safety is in the arms of Jesus and someday I am going home to Him. To be loved and cared for at last forever! Prayer helps me so much!

CHAPTER FORTY-TWO

L ife is a journey and will always be such. There is no GPS nor any road maps. There are always forks in the road. You make the best choice you can with the information you have at that time. Hindsight is 2020. And look at what the year 2020 brought! No-one gets out of life alive! I am no stranger to family drama, the vicissitudes of human nature or the disappointments and dangers life presents, but I have survived, perhaps even flourished at times.

I persevere, learning new things every day and temper it with a sense of humor. I know and acknowledge my limitations and try to accept them as such for today. Counting your blessings seems so trivial but really does put things into perspective.

I am blessed to be in a bungalow which is necessary for my physical limitations of my osteo-arthritis, essential tremor and fibromyalgia.

I am blessed all four of my kids are educated, have good jobs and are decent young people. Pretty damn good for a single parent!!!

I am blessed to have mental health resources to address my mental health concerns when I falter. Thanks David, Linda and Stefan! (I actually know 20 David's; each with a different role in my life.)

I am blessed to have professional knowledge of the services that should be rendered and the techniques that should be employed.

I am blessed to have a faith that takes away the fear of death, the faith that guides me daily and the faith God continues to protect me in ways I never imagined.

I am blessed to have an income and a food bank for when supplies when I run low.

I am blessed that I can drive to get myself out and about.

Thank God for the picturesque world around me. Thanks for my ability to see the beauty in each tiny thing except bees!!!!

Thanks to Dr. Metcalfe who sees me in person during Co-vid, listens, refers and works with me!

Thanks most of all for my sense of humor which ultimately leaves folks to wonder if I am nuts or just have a weird uncanny sense of humor!!!!

Most importantly I am blessed to have a rooster of close supportive friends: Karen, Margret, Bev, Trinkie, Wanda, Ashley, Colleen, Tracy, Tish, Trish, June, Mark, Rosanne, Angela, Stefan, Gulcan, Rosetta, Elizabeth, Doris, Bennie, Bernie, Jim, Hank, David, David, David, David and David. Please forgive me if I missed mentioning your name. Thanks for being my supportive system.

Thanks for believing in me and loving me. Thanks for the journey thus far!!!

It is what it is!!!
Via Con Dios

Printed in the United States
by Baker & Taylor Publisher Services